Shorts

Shorts

William R Long
M Div, Ph D, J D

ISBN: 978-1-7350927-9-9

Book Design by Sarah Katreen Hoggatt, Book Layout Biz
Printed in the United States of America

Contents

Introduction

THIS BOOK PRESENTS A NUMBER OF my current ideas in brief compass. It reflects at least eight different genres of writing and many distinct areas of inquiry. The genres are: short story, sermon, legal brief, a collection of aphorisms, a rhyming poem, historical and biographical essays, an exegetical exposition, theological essays. The opening piece, "Paragraphs," consists of ten pungent paragraphs describing ten features of life in contemporary America. I hope you find the following short pieces entertaining, challenging and inspiring. In keeping with the idea of the title, that is all I want to say. Happy reading!

I

A Few Short Paragraphs

1
Paragraphs

THE IDEA BEHIND THE FOLLOWING TEN paragraphs is that we increasingly form our opinions and approaches to almost everything these days almost instantaneously. Two seconds of looking up the answer to a question is now dubbed "research." Most people don't really read books anymore; we barely can get through a newspaper story. In keeping with our shorter attention span, I have written the following paragraphs. They are my attempt to address what I think are ten important issues in our culture today—one paragraph per issue.

A. The Intensification of Language. We communicate mostly with words, and we have an array of them, from coldly scientific to heatedly emotional, to get our meaning across. The culture of the twentieth century treasured and trained people in careful, calm, scientific and measured speech. That still is there, but increasingly our public language is taking on an intensity that seems to have no other purpose than to frighten—and then destabilize people. Words like "bombshell revelation" or "terrifying truth" or "shocking reality" or "stark warning" or "breaking news" fill the airwaves. We hear that our money is constantly at risk, as is our health and safety. No wonder everyone takes pills—and trusts no one. Who benefits from this?

B. Apocalyptic Language. This differs from the previous paragraph in that God is now thrown into the intensified sentences. God is certainly on the brink of planning something devastating unless people repent immediately. The end is coming soon. America's best days are behind us. Nothing but bleak days ahead. I think such people ought to be gathered up and quizzed and only permitted to continue speaking like this if they can show that they have had a long history of calling things right.

C. Enhanced Safety Consciousness. The big story of the late twentieth and early twenty-first century that you have never heard about is the growing centrality of the concept of safety in our society. Too many industrial deaths last century led to massive workplace changes. Changes to cars then followed suit. Helmets for many activities followed. Safety protocols sprang up galore. When anyone leaves for a trip we say two words to them we never said before 1980: "Be safe." Our society, by all objective measures, is safer now than at any time in the past. But we don't feel that way. Thus, there is a shadow side to safety—that we lose our bearings on how to determine what constitutes a danger. We are in that cultural space now.

D. Fear. Plato got into the act long ago on this subject by putting in Socrates' mouth in *The Republic* this definition of courage: "the preservation of the belief that has been inculcated by the law through education about what things and sorts of things are to be feared." That is, an intelligent, educated and courageous person knows that there are things to fear, even though one doesn't want to live one's life in fear. We don't have a process or consensus now to help us determine what there is to fear "out there." Maybe nothing. Maybe everything. We are clueless.

E. Baby Boomers. What the Baby Boomers will never tell Gen X or Gen Z or Millennials is that the American economic system *was rigged* in their favor. Boomers. They are now enjoying the fruit of a rigged system, and they think they deserve that fruit. A case in point is the pension system, the modern version of which arose in the 1960s. It set out generous levels of employer contributions that could be matched by employees. So generous, indeed, that many of those beaming Boomers today are living on a pension that far exceeds their top salary. But this "generosity" depleted the coffers of the companies and government, leading to massive scaling down of pension plans and salaries. The results? The Boomers buy all the new luxury homes; they pay cash; they bump and embarrass the Millennials and Gen X and Gen Z. And the Boomers think all is fine with the world. And the younger ones are getting more pissed by the day.

F. Conversation. Those who grew up between 1960-1990 knew that three conversational subjects were off limits in polite interaction: religious choice, political affiliation and sexual practices. The reason these were off limits was because people seemingly had their own take on these three things and this take was so unique to them that if someone really tried to push them on it, it would lead to an argument and even ruptured relationships. Thus, people knew how to keep the peace relationally and only tread on those subjects in the most protected and clearly-defined environments (a counseling session/a political gathering/a worship service). They talked about religion, sex and politics, but only in venues where they were encouraged to do so. We have lost that today, as political conversation has moved from private to public space. Everyone has his or her opinion, however weird, and people will let that opinion break relationships and fracture friendships. We will learn to put those conversational subjects back where they belong, but not until lots more people die and families break up because people happen to disagree in these areas and just can't keep their mouths shut.

G. Obesity. Let's face the truth: America is too obese. Blame it on the Pandemic. Blame it on food manufacturers who want to addict us to sugar or other unhealthy things. Blame others. Do all this if it makes you feel good. Until you look in the mirror and see an expanded version of yourself. The growing obesity crisis is the physical or outward face of an idea crisis in American life. We want freedom and that means we can get what we want. We want satisfaction and that means we get whatever food we want in whatever quantity whenever we want it. Do we have the capacity to reverse this? Or will we simply have to confine people for months or years on liquid diets until they look good again? Fat may sometimes be beautiful, but obesity isn't.

H. Religion. Religion is having a terrible, horrible, no good very bad day in America now. You might question that judgment and point to certain vibrant religious fellowships, but that wouldn't be wise. Our inability to do Letter F above properly has led to conflict galore in churches, except those that are so ideologically aligned politically that it is that political commitment that holds them together. But religion is a funny thing. It has been such a moving force in human history that every powerful movement, from politics to sport, wants to claim it. But religion will get the last laugh, as it shucks off these people like the farmer peels off and then discards the husk of an ear of corn. Religion is having a bad day because it is clothed with so much extraneous and strange stuff. It will one day have a comeback, but it has to wade through a lot of selfishness and stupidity before that can happen.

I. The American Dream. The problem with America now is NOT that young people don't want to work or that they are deficient in civics education but that they have too MUCH belief in America. James Truslow Adams, in his 1931 classic *The Epic of America,* made popular the phrase "the American dream." This dream was one in which "each man and woman shall be able to attain to the fullest stature of which they are innately capable. . ." Our problem is not that we have lost sight of this dream but that everyone wants it—NOW . What one generation thought should take a lifetime to achieve is thought by the current generation to take "three years Max." But it doesn't happen in that time. It almost never does. And people live disappointed lives. Envy skyrockets. Rents increase. Layoffs happen. People feel like failures. They aren't, but they feel that way, not because they don't love America but because they love the idea of America too much.

J. Periods of Life. On the American scene, Thomas Cole first proposed stages of life visually, through his four "Voyage of Life" paintings from about 1840. Gail Sheehy modernly picked up the notion literarily through her popular 1977 book *Passages.* It popularized an entire field of study, called "Life Course Research," which had just recently emerged. But then things became complex—people "divided" life in innumerable ways of varying lengths of time. Confusion set in. Let me remove the confusion. I say unto you--In America we generally live our lives in three periods: Training, Chaos, Freedom. The rest is commentary.

II

People You Should Know

The following three essays introduce you to four special people in my intellectual and professional life.

2

Jon and Lance

September 18, 2024

After the first three paragraphs, which may be off-putting because of my attempts at verbal dexterity, I get to the subjects of this essay: Jon and Lance. Please be patient.

I used to think that the primary long-term benefit of being a professor who wrote prolifically was that my written words would endure. I thought that people decades, if not centuries, from now would gratefully *pore* over my *palabras* and *linger longingly* over my *lugha* (it means "language" in Arabic). Fueling this sentiment was my love of the book of Job, a book in which Job expressed his deepest longing in these words (19:23-24): "23 Oh that my words were now written! oh that they were printed in a book! 24 That they were graven with an iron pen and lead in the rock forever!" I loved the intensity of those verses, especially the culminatory word, which provides an unexpected multilingual alliteration: *"chatsab,"* which means *"chiseled"* (translated here as "graven"). Thus, my expectations of permanence were deeply etched in my consciousness, and my writing continually fueled that hope.

But then, as time went on, I realized that that hope was nothing but a mirage, or something that looks like a shining and inviting body of water from a distance but which, upon arrival, has inexplicably dried up. This realization came through a number of experiences, but it left me in the unenviable position of looking at my words and realizing that they were as evanescent as a wisp of the prairie wind that I felt blow past me while writing this essay from a bluff overlooking downtown Kansas City. I yearned for permanence, but I realized that the thing I thought was most permanent was actually disappearing almost as soon as I wrote it. It was like the irony of storing all things permanently in the "cloud," which, last time I flew through them, parted more easily than the Red Sea before Moses.

All of this made me rather more glum than I usually am, and I wracked my brain to see if there was a redemptive way out of this dilemma. And then, it dawned on me. One of "gifts" of teaching, which I always appreciated but never really fully embraced, was that I had a few students whom I picked up either in the classroom or through years of interaction with students and teachers, who not only were very special to me but whom I felt were, in a special way, shaped by some of my thoughts and ways of doing things. It was not as if I focused much on the way this happened or patted myself on the back when I realized this. More powerful to me was my growing interest in the unfolding of *their* lives-- in their careers, in their mastery of technique, in their gradual rise in their fields, in their projecting their own voices far beyond the reach of my own weak *Wörter.* And then, when I began to think in these terms I was delivered from the dilemma of focus on the self, the self which Luther famously characterized as incorrigibly *incurvatus in se,* or "curved inwards towards the self." I began to think of them, the students and colleagues, the ones whom increasingly occupy my best thoughts waking or sleeping. I would like to tell you about two of them in this brief essay.

Jon and Lance

Though Jon and Lance are, of course, two distinct individuals, and quite different individuals at that, I often place them together in my consciousness. They were both students, Sophomores or Juniors I think, when I showed up to chair the history department and be a professor of history and government at tiny Sterling College in Sterling KS in 1990. I had come from teaching at a college that was on everybody's 'top ten' list for academic rigor; I was going to a college that was on no one's 'top thousand' list for the same. But it was at this 'lesser' place that the 'greater' relationships developed. And the ironies are compounded as I think of the two people I want to introduce: Jon and Lance. Jon, very conservative by nature, has spent his illustrious career getting paid millions from liberals (mostly school districts, largely influenced by left-leaning groups); Lance, very progressive by nature, has spent his equally luminous career pulling down millions from Midwest farmers who, last time I checked, weren't forming a PAC for Bill Clinton (when I was in Kansas) or Kamala Harris (in 2024).

First, Jon

Jon came to Sterling via a deep past in Pennsylvania but a more recent history in Arizona. He was a standout athlete in high school, and he would parlay that talent into athletic and academic achievement at Sterling. In fact, Sterling would become the gateway to his securing a position teaching special needs students in Virginia. Well, I don't want to get ahead of myself too quickly, so let me return to Sterling, where we first met. I was new; John was BMOC ("big man on campus"). His forceful manner and endearing personality enabled him, largely, to declare the "rules" of his academic engagement, and I saw how that worked when he stopped by my office the first week I was there, just before classes started in August 1990. Jon, who was a history major, kindly told me that I ought not to expect a lot from him for a while because he had "two-a-days" now and for the foreseeable future. Two-a-days was athletic slang for intensive practices both morning and afternoon, leaving the athlete physically and mentally depleted but stronger and more competitive.

That, at least, was the theory. So, Jon was kindly advising me not to put many demands on him in my classes because he was otherwise occupied. He was being kind, but he was also being direct, and there was no mistaking what was at stake was a sort of power dynamic between professor and student that I had previously met at my first teaching venue. What I said to him in one sentence ended up transforming the conversation and our relationship. I calmly looked at Jon and said, "Jon, great to meet you too, but if you are working with me you will be doing academic two-a-days." I said no more than that. Jon looked at me as if to say, "Don't you know who I am?" and then he trudged off, muttering under his breath something like "Right, academic two-a-days."

Thirty years later, when I was talking to him as he was planning his second multi-million dollar company, he said to me, "Dr Long, do you realize how many papers you made me write in the time I worked with you?" One should know that I came from teaching at a college that required students to write frequent short essays expositing classic texts. I answered: "I have no idea, Jon." He looked at me, with a combination of long-repressed frustration that was, in fact, tinged with admiration, "Seventy-seven!" Then he went on, "I wrote the best memos to my staff! No one ever doubted as to what they were to do, where the company was heading or what I expected of them. I never knew that Achilles dragging around Hector's dead body in the *Iliad* would make me into such a good writer." If I hadn't realized it earlier, I realized at that moment that what was most enduring about my professional life was that I was able to impart a very valuable skill to someone by repeated demands and accountability. Just to finish the story: after Sterling, Jon moved to Virginia and became a teacher of special needs students. This experience helped him see how the right words and attitude of a teacher could transform someone's life. But he had greater ambitions. He then realized that with the passage of a new law (dubbed "No Child Left Behind") under Bush II, that all kinds of students would become tested *ad nauseam* so that parents and others would have "data" on their child's achievements. So, Jon came up with the idea to hire dozens of teachers to write thousands of questions keyed in the most minute way to the hundreds of state academic achievement standards, and then sell that idea to school districts, first in Virginia and then beyond Virginia. His gridiron skills (building a team) and intellectual doggedness (some of which I may have contributed to) resulted not only in his company becoming Virginia small business of the year but in creating networks of relationships that are helping him today as he plans and implements his next company.

Then, Lance

Lance's situation coming to Sterling couldn't have been more different than Jon's. Lance is the son of Terry, a Presbyterian minister (the tradition of Sterling College is Presbyterian) who was educated at Sterling in the mid-1960s and then went to Princeton Seminary for ministerial training before diving into one of the roughest neighborhoods in Kansas City KS for a dozen year of ministry. Lance spent several years growing up in that neighborhood. Despite his utter familiarity with such a major urban center, Lance's deep roots, as is typical of most Kansans, are on a Kansas farm. Lance's was in far West Kansas, and its Western border in those days hugged the Eastern border of Mountain Standard Time. Thus, he was a kind of "bi-cultural" person by upbringing, easily relating both to urban and rural, with a calm and genial temperament that made him attractive to people from across the political spectrum.

We connected at Sterling, where he was also a history major, but in ways less dramatic than my initial conversation with Jon. Lance just appeared, hat askew, pen sticking out of his mouth, wanting to share with me the joys of his last bike ride across the windswept prairie, but eager to learn history and figure out how the complexities of urban, rural, faith, literature, history and so many other things could fit in one mind and one life. While I saw in Jon an enormously focused energy and true leadership capability, I saw in Lance a kind of quiet intellectualism, wonderful disposition, and a natural comfort with people urban and rural and everything in between. Jon would be a motivator, a direction-setter, a team builder; Lance would be a thought-leader, a patient friend who identified and steadily worked through people's problems in life.

Lance discovered, as he went on to complete two Master's degrees, that he was drawn back to the farm, the farm that had first inspired his imagination at age eleven when he started spending summers there to harvest, drive tractors, pluck corn freely from stalks and generally have a sense that his future was as unlimited as the Western Kansas sky. But Lance combined his training in dispute resolution and business, along with his personal experience on the farm, to land a job at the leading Midwest agricultural accounting and consulting firm. His steady disposition and genial manner quickly was noted, and he became the manager of a regional office in his early 30s. Then, Lance did something that Jon also did in about 2005—he reached out to me.

Jon wanted me to consult with him as he was planning his first company, but Lance wanted something else from me. He wanted so to polish his writing and speaking skills so that he might, one day, be a "thought leader" in the field of agricultural family business consulting. This might sound like "small business" with a small "s," but anyone who has the slightest awareness of agriculture in America knows that the smaller the business, the huger the issues. Lance wanted not only to be able to sit across the dining room table and talk to a family about the problems of succession and issues of fairness and equity but he wanted to be able to capture the emotions of people as they wrestled with these problems. A classic problem, for example, is when Child One has stayed on the farm and wants to inherit it (and expects to inherit it) but isn't really capable of running it, but Child Two has gone to the big city for education, is more capable and now wants to return to the farm to manage it. Lance effortlessly managed a staff of dozens at the big firm, but he wanted more. He also effortlessly brought new people into the business, building his team of consultants, but he wanted to be able to put his thoughts so precisely on paper and deliver them so powerfully from a podium that they would be remembered.

When Lance called me in 2005, ostensibly to get me to consult with a Kansas foundation on whose Board he sat (In the meantime I had gone to law school, been a litigation attorney and was then a law professor), we began a conversation that continues weekly almost twenty years later. He has achieved in his field the kind of deep relationships and trust so that people from the highest political and business echelons in the Midwest regularly call him. But we still work on those essays, trimming here, adding a thought there, polishing things so that they shine.

I now am basking in the reflected glory of these two students. They were in my classroom nearly thirty-five years ago, and I see them and their personalities in their work, of course, but I also see a little of myself. And both of these things give me immense delight. Thank you, Jon and Lance, for teaching me that the best result of teaching is, in fact, being a teacher, and seeing the fruit of that in your lives of service and accomplishment.

3

Then, There is Andrew

October 9, 2024

LITTLE DID I THINK THAT WHEN a friend, a retired judge in Oregon, introduced me to Andrew at a lunch nearly five years ago, that our professional and intellectual lives would become so deeply intertwined. There was little reason to think it would be so at first. He was spending some time in the Northwest but was a professor of history in South Carolina. He focused primarily on the experiences of Jews in medieval Spain and the broader European world, but he also had developed an impressive interest in the history of medicine. I, on the other hand was keeping up with an array of people (including Lance and Jon) and, after March 2020, devoting myself increasingly to my "pandemic projects"--a book of poetry or a few volumes on the origin of English idioms. At our second or third lunch Andrew almost casually mentioned to me that he had always been interested in studying Classical Greek but had only pursued that interest intermittently. Would I be interested in working with him to sharpen his Greek skills?

I had taught Biblical Greek more than forty years previously to several classes of Seminarians while I was pursuing my M. Div., and I had been "reading around" in Homer lately, but I had just that month come out with my book on Chinese love poetry and was, frankly, a bit out of practice in Classical Greek. But I said "yes," and he was pleased, and so we started "Zooming" twice weekly in the late summer of 2020 to study Classical Greek.

More than four years later we are still at it, and it has been one of the most exciting intellectual journeys of my life. Andrew is by far the most brilliant student with whom I have worked and combines with that intelligence a troika of "D" virtues—deferential, devoted, dogged—that has made our experience a true adventure of mind and spirit. I'll get to those in a moment, but first I would like to introduce you to him. He, though embracing his Jewish identity, readily admits that he is as much a scion of New England Puritanism as I. His origins are in the Boston suburbs, his intellectual drive was kindled early, and he attended Reed College in Oregon. I had begun my teaching career at Reed (one of our most significant points of connection), but I was teaching there more than a decade before he matriculated. His intellectual prowess was quickly recognized and, after Reed, he earned an M. Phil. at Cambridge in England before topping it off with a fellowship in Italy, a Ph. D. in Historical Studies from the University of Pennsylvania, and a post-doc at UCLA. His award-winning dissertation was turned into a book in 2015. He has complemented that with a more recent book, *The Land is Mine,* where he explores the world of a few Jewish Biblical commentators in Renaissance Spain on the subject of the importance of the rural experience. This is a salutary correction to much work on the history of the Jews, which focuses on urban spaces or classroom-type learning. Though the subject might appear arcane, Andrew has a writing style that is at both lucid and elevated, energetic and thoughtful, exploratory but focused. He has "checked all the boxes" academically and now is a Full Professor of History in South Carolina.

Yet, the fact that he wanted to try to learn Classical Greek as his 40th birthday present to himself, indicates that the mountain he has now set himself to climb is just as significant as the one around which he focused his academic training and which, no doubt, he thought would suffice to carry him his entire career. Learning ancient Greek starting at 40 is like a combination of a mature surgeon learning robotic surgery at 45 (as one of my friends did) and someone thinking that learning a slew of Eastern languages starting in his 50s (i.e., me) was the way to go. Ancient Greek is that vast, and it is that difficult.

So, we began to work together, twice weekly, working through two volumes of grammar before moving to reading of texts. I would do most of the speaking at the beginning, and I would gradually learn my role, from quizzing him on minutiae (such as forms of verbs or nouns/adjectives) to encouraging him to articulate and explore the intellectual and verbal worlds we were opening. We started our reading with Plato, as is usual, but then we "veered" off into some New Testament reading before reading extensively from the Septuagint. That our "curriculum" was fully unique can be seen in that we then moved to reading some of Galen's (second century CE physician) medical texts before turning to our present project—Marcus Aurelius' (second century CE Emperor) *Meditations.* We settled into rhythms of work that fit our schedules, and for each session Andrew comes prepared to translate, while I pepper him with questions, occasionally correct or improve or expand what he is doing and, increasingly, tell him that he is suggesting a better translation than mine. We also explore the idea worlds behind the text, reflecting on the development of medical terminology in antiquity or tracking down the Septuagint's use of a word or reflecting on central concepts of Stoicism through Marcus. Each day has yielded insights of value.

I thought at first that I was largely responsible for the "flow" and quality of our times but I have now come to think that he is. He is so because of the "three D's" I mentioned above. He is unfailingly *deferential*, and by this I mean he seemingly is elated when my translation explores avenues that he hadn't thought about. He is always open to my idea and textual suggestions, humbly accepting corrections when I bring them, gently persistent when he thinks he is "onto" something, always ready and prepared to work on the subject at hand. But he is also *devoted* to the work. I decided to use "devoted" rather than simply "dedicated" because "devoted" takes us into the interior spaces of the heart more fully than does "dedicated," and I know that the texts, the words, the ideas and the whole universe of the Greek world is something that not just attracts him but is giving him a new and inviting world in which to live. Finally, I say he is *dogged* because of the way he faces discouraging situations. Each new ancient Greek author presents us with almost a new language, an idiolect, and it is easy to become disheartened as one tries to enter into a new verbal and intellectual space. Andrew will face the challenges of Marcus, for example, his arcane words, his showy pleonasms, and will learn them, little by little, until he has the confidence to compare his translation with published translations and defend his own. But this takes a rare kind of tenacity that keeps returning to the sources, the *fontes,* and knowing that there is more to discover from them.

So, we continue our work together. He is now exploring ways to redefine himself and his intellectual interests in the whirlwind of contemporary social media and academic presentation apart from learned journals. On my better days I think that our twice-weekly meetings have encouraged him in this quest and given him the perspective of one "steeped" in the "old world of learning," a world we both share and appreciate. I am sure he hears my voice even when we don't meet. I, for one, receive new energy when we work together. The world seems to come alive in new and fresh ways in the hour we meet—and beyond. And, I have him to thank for it.

4

And Emily, Too

December 3, 2024

Of the many pleasures of my early 70s, one of the most unexpected is the deepening of relationships with highly talented and motivated people decades my junior. What I didn't realize until just a few years ago was that I had been long developing powerful mentor connections with people in their early 50s and 40s and, with Emily, a person in her late 20s. In this story I would like to tell you a little about her, how we became connected and the joy she brings to my life.

Whereas Lance is an agricultural family business consultant, Jon an entrepreneur and founder of companies, and Andrew a refined scholar of the history of medicine and the world of Judaism, Emily comes from a Catholic tradition and is in the final stages of her doctoral work in early Catholic theology. When I combine these folks with my Arabic work with my Muslim friend Iyad, Chinese with my Confucianist friend Juwen and Sanskrit with the Nepalese Hindu Daya, I feel like I could sing "We are the World" nearly every day of my life and be enriched with each singing. My deep engagement in the sacred traditions of the world, through the languages of the traditions that represent nearly 90% of the world's people, gives me a sense of rootedness and deep anchorage that is able to withstand, so far, the buffeting surface winds of contemporary political vagaries.

Well, this is all background to my connection with Emily who, with her energy, optimism, curiosity, intellectual fervor and pastoral heart brings joy to me as she invites me into the highways and byways of her intellectual journey into the fascinating world of Catholic legal and theological thinking. We connected early in 2018 thanks to the same judge friend who later introduced me to Andrew. The judge had been her high school Constitution Team coach when her school competed in the national championships about a decade ago. But she only entered into my life when she was a first-year law student in Kentucky, brooding over a choice (to pursue law) that she knew wasn't right but which she felt she needed to honor. Her Christian faith, which had always been of some importance to her, had taken on new dimensions of significance as a result of a Lenten Service in her senior year of college but since she had already committed to attend law school, she felt she had to follow that commitment.

But things didn't work. It wasn't that she didn't "get" the niceties of personal jurisdiction or the various categories of torts (that is NOT "tortes"); it was just that seeing the joy on other students faces as they parsed what constituted a "contact" for jurisdictional purposes simply left her empty. Her emptiness was enhanced when she attended first-year law classes in the old theological seminary classrooms and chapel (because the law school was being refurbished); it was almost as if theology was "calling" her but not permitting her to hear the call at the same time. Well, about that time I entered her life and we began weekly conversations about law, theology, how to extricate oneself from law school, how to think of theology as a discipline and career and how to make it all work so that bridges weren't burned and the psyche was intact. After taking a year off from law school, she decided to attend Yale Divinity School where she immediately dove into the courses with a rare fervor and focus. Every week I would listen as she recounted what she learned, ask her some questions about it, but encourage her to think of ways that her dual loves (theology and law) might become wedded as she continued to search for a focus in theology. She didn't want to stop with a Master's program, and so we talked through doctoral programs before she decided on Boston College in Chestnut Hill MA.

But as time went on our conversations, though still anchored in theology and law, increasingly became supplemented with "life" concerns. Emily possesses a fine sense of familial loyalty and the nuances that family can bring to life, and her depth of understanding, human sympathy, humor and good will have encouraged me to share things about my life that I would rarely tell another soul. So, our conversations covered a broad waterfront of topics. Then, about five years into our relationship, we decided to do some Latin work together. I told her mine was "rusty," but she seemed to "mishear" that as "robust" or something like that, and so we dove into the niceties of medieval Catholic theology on a work hitherto untranslated into English, though I did, I confessed to her, consult the German translation at times! We both were enriched as we felt ourselves exploring dimensions of the early Franciscan tradition that had not yet been written about but were basic to her evolving interest in the intersection of theology and canon law in medieval Catholicism.

Because she is now in her dissertation stage, our conversations are no longer weekly; she is in the good hands of a multi-national doctoral committee (Italian, English, American) which is stretching her in textual, linguistic, ethical, legal and theological ways that she wouldn't have thought possible a few years ago. I couldn't be more delighted at her progress. When we talk, the first thing we agree on is to limit our time to ninety minutes—and then we are off to the races. I feel rejuvenated by her energy and passion for learning and, in my reflective moments, I hope to have given her some support and guidance as she establishes her professional identity.

III

Short Stories

These are self-explanatory. The only thing I will say is that the ideas for them arose from my life experience, even though each one of them is largely fanciful.

5
Finding Her Body
June 10, 2024

He, whom we will simply call "the friend," hadn't heard from his friend Stephanie in several hours. This was unusual, and so rather than texting her endlessly he decided to stop by her home to see how she was doing. They had known each other for about four months, since Stephanie had moved to the Salem area to be near children and grandchildren. She was such an impressive figure in the town that it didn't take him long to notice her and find a way to ingratiate himself with her. Because of her confidence, ease of manner, sparkling beauty and approachable personality, he managed to secure a conversation and then a longer meeting with her. He considered himself fortunate to talk to and be seen with someone who obviously was the class of the town, even though she downplayed her striking blond features and shapely form.

As the months wore on they saw each other more and more frequently, taking day outings and attending night concerts at the local jazz club, which doubled as an Italian restaurant. He loved the combination of her vivacity and cheerfulness, her readiness to laugh at his jokes and the vague sense that she found him interesting, though he never actually discovered why she really liked or even tolerated him.

But all this came to a crashing end that June evening when she didn't answer her texts or phone. He quickly made his way to her home to see what, if anything, might be wrong. There was no answer at the front door, even after his insistent rings and knocks, and so he went to the side gate, unhooked it and entered. He thought he saw a recumbent form at the back of the property near where she had just been clearing kale plants and prickly vines in preparation for planting some small fruit trees and deliciously colorful flowers.

He rushed over to see what the distance only slightly revealed and was horrified to discover that the recumbent form he had only partially seen was indeed Stephanie, lying on her back with several prickly vines protruding from her arm, apparently lifeless. Blood had quickly escaped from the multiple cuts inflicted by the vines, and now it pooled into such a luxuriant redness that it reminded him, rather perversely, of the brilliant red pinot noir they had enjoyed together at jazz the previous Thursday evening. The panic of the moment, however, drew him immediately away from any thoughts of the jazz venue, as he saw that her once lifelike visage was now pallid; her neatly sculpted facial features had turned into a sort of marble or porcelain, and her stunning eyes into seeming glasslike mirrors now showing not the depths of the soul but simply a bland vacancy. Still, he thought, the quiet beauty even of her relaxed facial muscles would have made the heavenly cherubs jealous.

He quickly checked for a pulse and, alas, there was none. The blood, which had formed an extensive pool by the time he arrived, had obviously fully left her body, and all that remained was the lifeless, though angelic form, lying on the now bloodstained soil. He let out a shriek of pain and confusion. "My Stephanie!," he cried. He really didn't know for a second whether he should just say "Stephanie!" or "My Stephanie!" since their mode of personal engagement to date left certain ambiguities as to whether their relationship betokened a budding friendship, a nascent romance, or a simply a pleasant senior companionship. Yet, his problem of lack of clearly-defined relational boundaries didn't stop him from quickly calling 9-1-1 and then the emergency line of the police department, to try to get a detective and some investigating officers to the scene as quickly as possible.

Salem, Oregon, where they lived, was no stranger to sudden and inexplicable deaths, and it was uncertain at this juncture how Stephanie's would ultimately be characterized. There was no evidence of foul play, but he also was aware that there were sneaky and sinister ways for people to knock others off and make it look like a simple accident. Foul play, for example, was at the heart of a highly-publicized case where the body of the Director of the Oregon Department of Corrections was found outside of his office near the Oregon State Hospital, stabbed and bleeding to death. It was just outside the so-called Dome Building at the Oregon State Hospital, about a mile from Stephanie's house. Apparently the young Director, Michael Francke, had heard a noise outside his office in the gathering dusk, went to investigate, and was met by a knife-wielding person who slashed this promising, reformist-minding state worker to death. Indeed, Stephanie's death and that of the Director had certain eerie similarities, though there really was no time to go down that road at this juncture.

Two Salem police officers soon arrived, an interrogator and a detective, and the friend quickly ushered them to the backyard where they could witness for themselves the prone porcelain princess, who in life had been Stephanie. The detective went to examine the body while the other started interrogating the friend about the nature of their relationship. Apparently the interrogating officer had seen many cases of supposedly close friends knocking each other off in order to secure some kind of economic advantage, and so he looked on him, the friend, with suspicion. And then the friend started stumbling in his explanation of why he was there. It didn't redound to his credit when he couldn't really explain whether he was her acquaintance, friend, boyfriend or prospective suitor. Then, the detective investigating Stephanie's body stood up, looked the friend over and just said two words, "No way!" "No way, what?" was the friend's immediate response. The detective explained, "There is no way that a woman of THAT beauty would find a man like YOU to be boyfriend material! Just look at her." Then he began a description of Stephanie's body that bordered on the erotic as she lay supine, a slight smile creasing her lips. He continued. "The strength and surprising breadth of her shoulders, her wonderfully tapered form, narrow waist, noticeable breasts, and somewhat eye-catching backside all make me think that your ability to reel her in would have been like Captain Ahab trying to reel in Moby Dick—oops, bad metaphor! But you see what I mean."

The friend blanched and began to weep. Things were happening too quickly. He had lost a friend, a dear and capable person, and the officers were treating her like a piece of meat and him like a potential suspect. But he didn't have much time to nurse his emotional wounds as the interrogator began to barrage him with even more questions. "You said you found her dead here, with vines sticking out of her arm. Likely story. The look of this place makes me think she was an accomplished gardener who wouldn't have just slipped and, boom, she is dead! There has to be more to the story than that. Tell me more." The friend uncharacteristically paused in his explanation and finally the investigator, in exasperation, said, "Ok, buddy, we are going to have to search your car. Take me to it, now!" The insistent tone of the interrogator's voice made the friend forget the legal niceties of the *Miranda case* and its warnings, and in what situations it might implicate the search of a vehicle. His head was swimming in a pool of his own grief as his dear Stephanie lay deceased in a pool of her own blood, and so he meekly complied with the interrogator's request. While they retreated to his car, the detective was snapping pictures that the friend was sure would be sold on the internet by the end of the day. He had vaguely heard of some semi-porn internet site called "Death Grip," where dead bodies were displayed in various stages of undress for money. Every fiber of the friend's being wanted to scream out that this was

WRONG but he saw that he was helpless and had to comply with the interrogator's demand. As they walked to his car, the detective then retreated to the police van to get a stretcher, obviously to whisk the body away for closer examination.

Then it hit the friend. He had, at Stephanie's request, gone to an upscale market to buy her some fresh jicama, had taken it home and cut some of it up. But because he wasn't sure which knife to use, he had taken his cutting knife and a more menacing meat cleaver, put them in the bag with the jicama and then loaded them all into the trunk of his car before coming over to visit Stephanie. So as they approached the car, a fresh panic hit him. They would open the trunk, find the bag, and inside the bag would be not just one, but two deadly knives in a bag. He was almost beside himself with grief and anger, and he now saw in a flash how his life would end. But he had no choice as the interrogator guided him to his car. Just before opening the trunk to find the telltale bag, he recalled one other fact that no doubt would seal his doom. Because of his near panic at Stephanie's not answering his texts, he had quickly loaded the bag with jicama, the knife and meat cleaver, but had forgotten to clean off the knife from its previous work of slicing tomatoes. So, as one could have predicted, the interrogator forced the friend to open the trunk, reveal and open the bag, and there was a large sharp knife, running with a red substance, and a meat cleaver. Presto! Case solved!

The friend let out another shriek of grief, but this time it was for himself. An hour ago his life was going well, but now it was in complete shambles, and there seemingly was nothing he could do to redeem it. The interrogating officer was speaking into his shoulder mic and proudly proclaiming that he had found the "perp," before guiding the friend back to what was now being characterized as a 'crime scene.' Tears were streaming down the friend's face as he realized how his life, as well as that of dear Stephanie, had changed in a moment of time. By the time they retreated to the back yard, the detective had secured Stephanie's body to the rolling bed, with straps around her shoulders and waist. Her face was still creased with the odd but endearing smile as the two officers quickly held informal court in Stephanie's backyard. The interrogating officer had also now secured the friend's arms with handcuffs. The friend was now nearly inconsolable, crying for himself, his own children, for Stephanie and her beautiful Salem family. Everything had turned to dust. Then he turned to get one last look at Stephanie before they led him away. But, in the commotion where the officers backs were turned because they still were in conversation, apparently one of the springs of Stephanie's bed had snapped and, to his surprise and chagrin, she had sprung up as if to meet him so that their faces were now just inches apart. "Stephanie!" he cried once again, as her lifeless but luscious lips luridly lunged toward his lips. The last thing he remembered was that their lips touched for an instant. It was their first and last kiss. She was lifeless, and he was in shackles.

6

Finding His Body

June 15, 2024

THERE REALLY WAS NO REASON WHY his body should have been found by anyone. At 72, he seemed to be the perfect picture of health. In addition, he had no known enemies; he managed to avoid large busses and trucks while crossing streets and generally lived an inconspicuous life in the capital city of a Western state. The only problem that he faced was a small health concern that was a gift of the medical profession rather than anything he had done or faced in the process of aging. About three years previously, his podiatrist had recommended he get bunion surgery to straighten out the toes on his left foot and he, being generally trusting of the profession, went along. But the surgery went slightly awry and in addition to getting somewhat straighter toes, he was bequeathed a heartbeat twice the legal limit, with atrial flutter, and a severe case of sleep apnea. He didn't understand any of this, having lived a healthy life previously, but the combination of an irregular heartbeat and difficulty breathing while sleeping tended to put a crimp into his neatly ordered life.

So, he pursued a dual strategy to deal with the issues. On the one hand he lined up a cardioversion procedure to get the heart beating regularly again, and within range of historic limits, and then he secured a large and awesome-looking machine that blew air into his nose so that his air supply would be unhindered throughout the night. But the "cost" of this latter strategy was that he had to wear a mask, connected to a gangly hose. He generally felt like he was hooked up to a hostile device for seven or more hours a day. He went along with this, even though it severely impinged upon his life. The medical establishment mumbled something about "aging" and dodged another bullet in its quest to try to provide some kind of care to people while avoiding responsibility for its mistakes.

This all worked adequately enough until his healthcare provider changed medical suppliers, and he now had to work through another system to acquire replacement parts for his sleep device. It proved to be an immense challenge because when he called to order equipment and supplies, the people on the other end of the phone spoke a language that only partially seemed related to English, and his knowledge of Gujarati or Uzbek or whatever their native language was, was not sufficient enough for him easily to switch competently into technical words in those languages, and so he was confined to English in his quest for replacement parts.

All this would not have been a problem had not his need for a replacement machine become extreme. His old machine was expiring and he, in order not to expire, ordered a new machine. But the medical device supplier had only started working with his health provider after he had acquired his initial supplies, thus requiring a completely new customer setup with the new company. Thankfully, he had secured a letter from his medical provider authorizing his order of new equipment. But because there was such a thing as human nature and mixed signals, the letter wasn't accepted by the supplier, and he was told to get another signature in order to activate his account. This was impossible in the modern medical community, since he had never actually met his own sleep doctor, having only worked with a battery of lower level technicians who told him dire stories of what happened if he forgot to use his equipment. So, he doggedly tried to use the letter that was provided to him by the doctor to convince the supplier that he needed new equipment. Didn't work.

Finally, on the third try, and after he pointed out the letter talked about "medical necessity" and that it had the printed signature of the doctor, the supplier relented and grudgingly agreed to supply a new device. But just as birthday cakes come with boxes and candles and lighters, so his new breathing device would come with countless other things—five things in fact. There would be a carrying bag, a set-up kit, various filters and hoses and the device or machine itself. So, he finally confidently placed an order that one of the people barely speaking English said was fine. He didn't know if she said this to get rid of him, since he was getting more and more agitated as the process dragged on, or whether the devices actually would be mailed to him, but he was a hopeful man, and so he believed they would be sent. The only problem was that his health condition was deteriorating by the day because the old machine had given up the ghost and the new one hadn't yet arrived. His sleep was terrible; his breathing was labored and he felt increasingly vulnerable.

Then, finally, one day he received a delivery, and was overjoyed! But, upon inspecting it he saw that it wasn't his new machine after all but just a new mask. He already had a mask like the one he received, and so he was chagrined and getting angrier by the day because he felt that one of the people who had trouble with English had told him his order was accepted. But the mask would be of no use. So, he responded in two ways. He first wrote a long note to customer service, complaining about the poor service and his need for the devices that his doctor had approved. Then, he called the customer service hotline once again to speak to another person, this time seemingly of East Asian origin, about his situation. The person with whom he spoke betrayed no hint of sympathy or understanding, but was kind enough to say that, of course, the five devices or items that were ordered would be coming in multiple mailings because they came from different places. Of course, shouldn't he have known that? He orders a piece of equipment; five things are sent; and they are from an undetermined number of places. His angry note to customer service was answered in a similar, and curt, way. The brief tone of it was, "You dummy, of course the stuff is coming on different days in different weeks from a number of different places. Just be patient."

Well, his rage was increasing as his health deteriorated, but still he clung to the hope that springs eternal in the human breast. But instead of hoping for Casey's getting to the bat, he was hoping that the mailing(s) would come. Finally, he received yet another email from customer service telling him that the delivery would happen that very day. It didn't say how many deliveries would take place or what was contained in the delivery, but simply that it would come that very day. The excitement began to build in him as he decided to stay around his apartment all day waiting for the Fed-Ex truck. Finally, late in the afternoon, he spied the Fed-Ex truck in the parking lot! Only when the angel came to Mary the mother of Jesus with news of the Savior's birth was joy in the world more intense. He rushed down to the parking lot, and the driver was still in the vehicle. He interrupted the man and, trying mightily to control his emotions, just said, as calmly as possible, "I am XXX; do you happen to have a package for me?" He asked the question even though he KNEW the answer was "Yes." He KNEW he would be breathing regularly in an hour, and that sweet repose and restored health were right around the corner. The Fed-Ex driver, who introduced himself as "Daniel," looked calmly at his clipboard and then at him, and said, "No, no delivery for you." "What???" was the panicked response of the sufferer. "I received a message that the Fed-Ex truck would be bearing packages for me." 'Nope," said Daniel. Before panic had fully set in, Daniel said, "There is another Fed-Ex driver in the area; perhaps he has it in his truck."

The sufferer didn't know whether to laugh or cry; to expire on the spot or try valiantly to keep up the ritual of breathing for a little longer. He asked Daniel, "Do you know the name of the other driver?" Daniel responded, "Yes, Daniel." All of a sudden a kind of vertigo overtook the customer, and he wondered for a moment whether he was a victim of a cosmic joke, spun out for him by people barely speaking English in cahoots with drivers named Daniel. Still trying to maintain a shred of dignity, he asked Daniel, "Well, can you call the other Daniel now, just to see where he is and whether he has my packages?" Daniel (the driver) said, "No, I can't. I don't know his number." "What??" The customer was in danger now of dying from apoplexy, as he wondered why Daniel couldn't reach Daniel. He KNEW this had all the markings of some kind of huge joke. Daniel explained, "Well, you have to understand the nature of the contracts that Fed-Ex has in this city. We work for different contractors and are only using the Fed-Ex trucks to make deliveries. We don't work for the same company." The customer, with extensive training in law, didn't want to go into the niceties of contractual relationships between drivers, suppliers and large companies, but was simply overwhelmed now with grief. Daniel was now pointing to another Daniel, an elusive Daniel, whom he believed probably existed, but was not in the area and that this Daniel couldn't reach.

The sufferer quickly withdrew from Daniel (whom we shall now call Daniel 1) and took off walking the streets. Perhaps the hookers and those suffering from mental distress, who seemed to hold daily conferences around his apartment, would be better company than any possible Fed-Ex driver named Daniel. He grew more and more inconsolable as he trudged up one street and down another. He wanted to find Daniel 2 and the elusive Fed-Ex truck more earnestly than Diogenes wanted to find an honest man. When he was just about ready to abandon hope, he spotted it! Another Fed-Ex truck was just pulling into a business about 500 feet away. Joy! Rapture! He set off at a sprint, like a refugee trying to evade guards as he fled to the border for his freedom. He drew near to the Fed-Ex truck; it started to move. He thought he could stop it, but it pulled away.

He was able to bang on the sides, but the truck just pulled away from him, heading down the road near his apartment complex.

Exhausted now, he started off on a jog towards where he had seen the truck. He rounded a corner and, to his great surprise, he saw the two Fed-Ex trucks now next to each other in front of another business. No doubt Daniels 1 and 2 were having a high-level summit on the future of the Middle East or something of that nature. He looked in one of the trucks—no one. Then, he looked in the other, and there was an unfamiliar man. He almost screamed the name: " Daniel???" A look of terror creased the face of the driver, as he realized that he might be facing an escapee from a nearby mental institution. He reached for his phone, no doubt to call for police backup, but then the sufferer just asked Daniel, "Hello, do you happen to have a package for XXXX?" Actually, he needed about three or four packages, he thought, and they may be coming from different places, but he was trying his best to convince Daniel 2 of his sanity. To his complete surprise, Daniel 2 looked at his log and said, "Yes, two packages for you." The sufferer didn't know if this meant that all his equipment had arrived and was in the two shipments, or whether his life was dangling before his eyes while filters came in one mailing, tubes in another, the carrying bag in a third and the machine in the fourth.

He quickly checked the labels on the boxes and decided that one of them had the coveted and valuable machine. Yes! He would be able to breathe again. He would be able to live. So delighted was he that he quickly signed for the packages. He would have given the guy his social security number and access to his investment account if he had demanded it. He took the two packages and set off at a quick walk to his apartment. So excited was he, however, that he broke into a jog and then a sprint. He had the packages of life! But all the stress was beginning to bear down on him now, and as he got to the elevator leading to his floor he felt a peculiar weakness and emptiness in the head, as if something vital had been taken from him. But he powered through, clutching the package, especially the package containing the machine. He clutched it to his chest with more devotion than the most sincere Madonna in Renaissance Painting clutched the Christ child. Soon he got to his door, but then it hit him. Though he held the package tightly, his senses left him. The last memory of his life was a fumbling attempt to fit the key into the lock.

Neighbors found his body a few hours later. The Jaws of Life were called in to try to disengage his hands from the box containing the breathing device, but the Jaws were unsuccessful. No doubt he was simply demonstrating the lesson he learned from his mother early in life, which was that once you get a good deal, you simply don't let it go.

7
The Great Dog Breakout of 2024

For My Daughter

September 11, 2024

CINDY, AN ENTERPRISING PROFESSIONAL FROM THE Northwest, decided during the Pandemic to get a dog. Many, many women made that same decision, a decision perhaps driven not only by a desire for companionship but also because of a need for full admiration and support from another living being. So, after shopping around, Cindy settled on a Cairn Terrier, whom she named Theo. I suppose it was her positive memories of Kansas as a child and the fact that Toto in the Wizard of Oz was a Cairn that influenced her decision. In any case, Cindy settled comfortably into the role of a dog-owner and diligently did the things that made life work for both of them.

Though Theo wasn't an overly affectionate dog, he was fierce, he was very smart, and he was loyal. He would faithfully wait for Cindy to appear home from work or shopping, and then would eagerly lap at her fingers as if Cindy offered both the bread and water of life simultaneously to him. Their relationship included Theo's curling up near her in the evenings to watch movies together, as well as perching atop the couch to report on any unusual movements in the neighborhood.

One day, however, Cindy began to notice something unusual in Theo's behavior. Though his interest in television and movies had been mostly lukewarm to date, Theo began to devote more and more attention to Cindy's programs and especially the movies she watched. But it wasn't just any movies. Cindy observed him closely and realized that Theo went on highest alert and manifested greatest interest when Cindy watched "prison" or "prisoner" movies. Indeed, Theo's favorites seemed to be two: *Escape from Alcatraz* and *Shawshank Redemption.* As Cindy repeatedly watched the latter, Theo's behavior would change. He would sit up alertly and began to bark, sometimes wildly, at the screen. He especially seemed to love the scene where the corrupt warden came into Andy's cell and discovered that Andy had escaped through a gaping hole in the wall, dug patiently over many years. When the warden's face fell, Theo's lit up, and he barked with unfeigned delight at the plight of the hapless warden. In a word, Theo loved the tale of a prison escape.

This would all have been well and good had Cindy not decided to visit her family a few hundred miles away and taken Theo with her. But during the visit Cindy became very busy and had to check Theo into a dog kennel for three days. The kennel was called the "Dog Yelp," perhaps as a way of trying to catch dog-owners' attention in the crowded marketplace of doggie day-care options in town. Cindy dropped Theo off at the "Dog Yelp" with some trepidation, because she never had let him out of her care previously, but she was encouraged when the staff said that there were web cams where she could always keep watch on precious little Theo if she wanted.

Well, Theo didn't want to go to the Dog Yelp. He barked and pulled away and even tried to run away from Cindy before she turned him over to the manager of the kennel. That manager, named Courtney, loved dogs and vowed to treat each dog as if it were her own. Though this satisfied Cindy, it made Theo very angry. He simply didn't want to be confined in some Dog Yelp with dozens of other dogs whom he didn't know. When Cindy dropped him off, Theo went to a corner of the room and pouted.

A few hours later Cindy began to feel a bit guilty for "abandoning" her "little baby," who was now about three years-old, at the Dog Yelp. She had vowed not to look at the web cams, lest the sight of her poor dog alone there evoke so much sympathy that she simply would drive over to pick him up. But finally, she could take the pressure no longer, and so she cautiously looked for Theo on the web cam. She was surprised at two things. First, the Dog Yelp was seemingly much bigger than she thought. There were separate rooms for "big dogs" and "smaller dogs" and "hyper dogs," and the total population of the place was perhaps 150 dogs. Dogs could freely pass from one room to the other, but they seemed to know their "place" in the scheme of things. Second, she looked in vain in the "smaller dog" room for Theo and, actually, began to panic a bit, until she decided to switch on the other room web cams and found Theo milling around the big dogs. She thought this was odd, but what was especially odd was when she saw Theo seemingly sidling up to the big dogs, as if in a conversation, and pointing out things to them with his paw. Cindy became fascinated with Theo's actions and wondered what he possibly could be communicating to some of these larger dogs. They were standing around, dumbly looking at Theo, but he was earnestly getting and holding their attention.

Well, the daily routine of the dogs had been explained to Cindy when she dropped Theo off. Five staff were there from 6 a.m. – 5 p.m. Then, the staff would feed the dogs and all but Courtney would then leave and go home. It was Courtney's task to prepare the dogs for the night and make sure they were all in their cages at 7:00 p.m. It was never a problem, since the dogs were usually tired after a long day and wanted to get back to their cages.

But this very night would bring a most dramatic and unexpected event. The most dramatic thing we would learn was that when Theo was milling around with the big dogs he wasn't just sniffing for smells; he was plotting revolution. He wasn't just trying to strut his stuff; he was recruiting the "big boys" for the boldest breakout in dog kennel history. In addition, while walking around the room where the "hyper" dogs were kept, Theo had noticed a small breach in the wall, almost invisible, in the corner of the room. He could see daylight beyond the tear in the wall, and he knew the staff would soon be repairing it. But with his very strong cognitive abilities, which ran in the "family" of Cairns, he decided to "recruit" the three Jack Russell terriers in residence, point out the little hole and tell them that, at a pre-arranged signal, they would furiously dig at the wall to make the hole bigger. Of course the Jack Russell's, premier digging dogs, were salivating at the thought of tearing up a wall or digging through a floor.

As Cindy watched the various web cams further, it dawned on Cindy what Theo was doing: he was recruiting the "big dogs" for the dangerous task of a breakout. In order to do this, however, Theo also knew that Courtney had to be "subdued" in some way, and he knew also that the smaller dogs had to be enticed or encouraged to leave through the hole in the wall that the Jack Russells were enlarging. So the "big dogs," which included a few Great Danes, several German Shepherds, and a few snarly Pit Bulls, were actually being recruited by Theo to do their nefarious work of aiding the dog breakout.

All was in readiness, as Theo continued to chafe under the restrictions of being confined at the Dog Yelp. Promptly at 6:00 p.m. one night, when the rest of the staff had left for the night and just before Courtney was about to start locking dogs in cages, Theo gave the signal. Two giant Great Danes leaped to their feet, walked over to Courtney and actually knocked her down. She screamed, but she realized that she had no one who was going to come to her aid. But this had never before happened in the annals of dog kennels, and so Courtney was totally unprepared for this assault. Her cell phone was in the other room, and she couldn't get to it. As she tried to extricate herself from the Danes who knocked her down, a few furry Labs, which usually were so friendly, actually jumped on her in apparent affection but the effect was to knock her back down. Then these so-called friendly Labs put their bodies over her, pinning Courtney to the ground, so that she was starting to suffocate. Satisfied that things were starting well, Theo then gave the signal to the three Jack Russell terriers who just couldn't wait to start digging. Dig they did and like Uma Thurman in *Kill Bill 2*, whose burrowing skills were especially important when she was buried alive in a coffin, so the Jack Russells bit, clawed, and scratched at the vulnerable wall until larger and larger chunks of daylight were visible.

The dogs were in an uproar but Theo, now perceived by all as the ringleader, calmed them, and directed them to march over to the wall and get ready to escape. Courtney, meanwhile, was still on the ground, struggling vainly against the two hundred or more pounds lying on her face and upper body. Soon she would lose consciousness because the Labs were lying across her face but, being gentle dogs, they made sure that Courtney would just lose consciousness from lack of breath and not die.

As Courtney was vainly thrashing about, trying unsuccessfully to free herself from the weight of the Danes and Labs and Shepherds, a queue of dogs lined up near the widening breach of the wall. Perhaps channeling his own anger, Theo had instructed them to go in groups to wreak havoc on the town. The first group which escaped, led by a pair of Dobermanns, headed for a nearby local bar, the "Slammer Tavern." The second group, led by two Malamutes and a Tibetan Mastiff, headed directly for the ball field, where a little league game was underway. A third group, led by two more German Shepherds, began to walk across a busy downtown street, bringing traffic to a screeching halt.

So, as the scene was unfolding, there was both tremendous chaos and order at the same time. From the perspective of the innocent civilians, it was nothing but chaos as they witnessed the escaped dogs beginning to march or run at them, disrupt their activity and scare them. The Dobermanns broke into the tavern, barked loudly, got people screaming and panicked, and forced them to flee, drinks in hand, to the parking lot. Then the patrons dashed or drove away in terror. The same thing happened at the little league field. Little Spider Jones, the nine year-old all-star, was at the plate when he was set upon by a Malamute and knocked down. A woman fainted. Men screamed. The game was hastily cancelled and people rushed in panic to their cars. Bedlam, rather than order, was taking over this mid-sized Northwestern city.

But it was the next two things that really set the city on edge. Another huge pack of dogs, numbering in the dozens and led by the German Shepherds, began to block a major urban intersection and refused to move. Stunned motorists got out of their cars until they realized that their lives might be in danger. But they couldn't move, and so they sat cowering in their vehicles while the dogs circled their cars and made menacing sounds. Police were called, and they rushed to the busy intersection, but one officer made the mistake of pulling his gun and threatening to shoot a dog. This evoked such ire among the citizenry that one woman said in a loud voice, "You shoot that dog and you are next, you pig!" Never before had the officer witnessed such treatment, especially at the hands (or mouth) of a respectable middle-aged woman. But soon the police had backed down and cowered in the corner, realizing that they couldn't force the dogs to do anything.

Pandemonium was gradually overtaking the city, but Theo still saved his most dramatic move for last. Along with a posse of about twenty other sturdy dogs, led by the fiercest Pit Bulls you can imagine, Theo dashed over to the City Hall, where the City Council was just beginning its evening deliberations. The doors to the chamber were open, but were watched by two burly guards, who menacingly surveyed the citizens who entered. But they weren't prepared for the Pit Bulls. One of the dogs, Bobby, took off after one guard and bit him squarely in the ankle, bringing him crashing to the earth in pain. The other Pit Bull, Barney, did the same to the other guard. When the officers lost *their* footing, the City Council realized that something else was afoot, and then, when they looked up, they were inundated by about two dozen dogs, barking, yelping and seemingly ready to attack them. The City Council members screamed; the Mayor blanched, and all quickly abandoned the chambers.

This left the unusual situation where two injured security guards were nursing their wounds as the dogs realized that they now were in charge of the City Council meeting. Unbeknownst to the dogs, the Council deliberations were being televised, and now the world, or at least the world of the city, saw, instead of Mr. Mayor and his dignified Council, dogs walking over the podiums, peeing in the aisles, taking over the most sacred venues of the public square. And, in the middle of it all was Theo. When all the counselors had fled, Theo clambered up into the Mayor's chair, looked around with a self-satisfied glance, picked up the gavel and rapped it (he watched this in the movies, too), and tried to get his fellow dogs to quiet down. In a word, the dogs now had taken over the city.

Cindy now was watching all of this from her mother's home in town with growing consternation. Now it was clear to her why Theo was such a rabid fan of jailbreak movies. He was planning his own! And, she knew she and she alone could now do something about this. So, she clambered into her car, drove the half-mile to the city council chambers, walked in, caught Theo's eye and simply said, "That's enough for one day, Theo. Want a treat??" Theo saw her holding out some of his favorite sweets and quickly dropped the gavel. He rushed off to Cindy who quickly put him in the car with the words, "We need to get out of here Theo and not show ourselves until things blow over." With that, they headed to the freeway and returned to Cindy's city. Thus ended the great dog breakout of 2024.

8

Rescuing the Cat

July 17, 2024

I awoke with energy on a cool July day. We had been suffering through an increasingly common summer heat wave in these parts, but the previous night turned colder, and I finally got several solid hours of sleep. After tidying up, I walked towards my kitchen but, before arriving, I saw a handwritten paper note under my front door. Damn! It's probably the management company harassing me for being too good a tenant, I thought. But rather than just crumpling it up, I decided to read it. Before reading the content, my eye fell upon the name at the bottom: Molly. Everyone knows a few Molly's, but the one who came immediately to mind was not someone I wanted leaving me notes under my door at 6:30 a.m. As is my wont, I thought the worst, imagined that this secret stalker had gotten inside the building and was ready to pounce on me when I opened the door. But then, I decided to read the note. It said that there was a scared cat perched outside the balcony of my third-floor apartment on a narrow metal ledge, and it was in danger of falling. I rubbed my eyes and wondered if it had come to this: that Molly so wanted to get back into my life that she would use the emotional hook of a stray cat to try to get my attention.

But the phone number on the note looked unfamiliar, and then I realized that it was written by my neighbor Molly who lives with her husband Gus in the apartment directly below me. She and he are an accomplished couple in their mid-40s. He is recovering from serious back surgery, and she has been tending him with expert care that would have made Florence Nightingale envious. I decided to check my balcony and, sure enough, bunched up in a little ball, gripping a very narrow metal bar, with alternating gray, white and black streaks was a well-groomed American Shorthair cat. Our eyes met, and I could see the palpable fear in the cat's eyes. My balcony fence was too high to reach over to get it, and the openings in the fence were seemingly too small for the cat to clamber through, and so we just looked at each other for a second: the cat pleading and me sort of shrugging my shoulders.

I knew I needed help, and so I called Molly, who quickly answered her phone. You learn things about people when you are faced with danger or an unusual situation, and Molly readily told me that the two things that most bother her in life are overthrow of nations and the comfort of cats. I told her I saw the cat fearfully clinging to the narrow metal bar, and she said, "I'll be right up." Of course, she brought a carrying case for the cat, and a full meal of liquid and solid food, lest our furry friend, while waiting for rescue, might be deficient in caloric intake. Molly immediately recognized the dilemma but thought that she could coax the cat to climb up under the fence, where there was a three or four inch gap between fence and concrete. No German lullaby composed to calm the most recalcitrant or distressed child was ever more sweet than Molly's voice as she tried to lure the cat to safety. But the cat wasn't buying it. Rather, the cat tried to wedge itself between the balcony and the siding of the apartment, a narrower space, because it was at eye level. A slight sigh came from Molly's lips as she realized we might have a cat with head stuck between fence and building. Molly, though, was unfailingly optimistic and positive, regaling the cat with epithets reserved for the most intimate of lovers, but still the cat wouldn't respond to her. We looked down and both concluded that if the cat fell it would be in real trouble though the morbid side of me tried to imagine whether the cat would land on its feet before crashing to the sidewalk below.

We also took a break for a minute to figure out next steps and mused on how the cat could have gotten there in the first place. We studied the façade of the building and realized there was a narrow ledge leading from fourth-floor apartments to the space above mine, and we opined that our cat had gingerly picked its way along this ledge looking for whatever cats look for in the dead of night. While we were trying to figure things out, Molly decided she would begin knocking on neighbors' doors to see if the rightful owner could be located. But then we ran into the reality of 2024 in America, where young people, who disproportionately reside in the building, look at 7:00 a.m. as the new 3:00 a.m., and didn't answer their doors. She returned in frustration. Then, we decided on a desperate scheme. Molly would reach through the fence as best she could, try to grab the cat around the neck while avoiding potential threatening claws, and then lift it up as far as she could. I would then reach over the fence down as low as I could and see if I could hang onto something of the cat to bring it to safety. We didn't hold a prayer meeting before we did this, though that wouldn't have been out of the question. Molly skillfully reached through, grabbed the cat and raised it. At the same time I reached down and yanked it by the head hairs and ears. I apologized to the cat, but told it I was also saving its life.

I gingerly brought the cat up over the fence and dropped it on the balcony, where Molly's feast of dry and liquid food was soon consumed by our furry feline friend. Molly's visage, which had gone from concerned, to desperate, to teary to determined, was now full of relief. Another cat saved. Life could return to normal. And, by the way, we found the owner, on the fourth floor, near the end of the building. The owner said something about inadvertently leaving her balcony door open the night before ….

9

Disaster at the Tailgating Party

For My Son

November 30, 2024

A QUICK CHECK OF NEWSPAPER HEADLINES IN the Fall tells us that one of the most popular sports in post-Pandemic America is college football. The season starts in the warmth of the late summer sun, gradually progresses into the crimson, golds and multi-hued yellows of the Fall leaves, and then ends in the cold and rainy days of late November. The excitement generated by watching one's team play is palpable. But, as I am gradually beginning to realize, the real excitement on game day is driven more by activities surrounding the game and not necessarily by the game itself. Or, to put it differently, the game is an excuse for exploring other types of excitement and excess. Girls get dressed up in the team colors, skillfully applying makeup to visible body parts to imitate an eagle or warrior or duck or husky or whatever the mascot might be. The guys wear jerseys of their favorite players, though frequently they are the jerseys of past heroes who are now in their mid-40s.

For years the reality of attending a game was simply dressing up, showing up, cheering up and then going home after the game.

But beginning about a generation ago, the new reality of tailgating entered the picture. Historians of the game will try to argue that tailgating really goes back to the Civil War, but it is the reality of new technologies--in freezers, grills and generous sedans—that have made modern tailgating possible.

Tailgating before the game, rather than the game itself, is now the focus of the day for many. People gather hours before the opening kickoff to sup and consume all manner of unhealthy foods and beverages as they allegedly prepare for the big contest for which they may not show up until well into the second quarter. It is a wonderful time for socialization but, truth be told, it often separates more than connects many people. On one occasion, for example, when I was in Palo Alto CA for a classic matchup between the Oregon Ducks and Stanford Cardinal, I happened to attend both tailgates. The Oregon one had guys drinking kegs of beer and wolfing down greasy burgers and fries with gusto, while the Stanford one had guys in tortoise-shell glasses, white shirts with sweaters draped around their shoulders, wearing various kinds of Birkenstocks and sipping different varieties of wine supplied by vintners they had rented for the day.

But that was 2014 and since then tailgating has grown to be a national sport. They even have a drawing at halftime at some games for the "best tailgater," though the criteria for earning that award are somewhat nebulous. The reward? More food, adding to the obesity crisis that grips people, though the crisis is largely ignored on game day. Well, people tailgate in parking lots, near Alumni Centers, wherever one can pitch a tent and have access to food. And all usually goes well.

Until … the disaster tailgate of 2024. Let me set the context. I was in Corvallis Oregon, the home of Oregon State University. Corvallis is one of the most underrated towns in America, generally ignored but charming in nearly every way. It has no interstate passing through the town, though it is the home of one of the major research universities on the West Coast. The amenities that go with that are abundant levels of federal funding as local versions of the EPA or the Forest Service or various other agencies are scattered throughout the town. In addition, since OSU is the state land-grant university, going back to Civil War-era legislation, it houses all the agricultural programs for the state. One might think that agriculture is "dying," but it is very much alive in Corvallis.

Which leads to the issue of the day. OSU had been a credible and creditable presence in the PAC-12 Athletic Conference for many years but, with the recent breakup of that conference when big dollar signs were dangled in front of the Oregon Ducks (which really doesn't need more money after what Nike-founder Phil Knight has given to the school) and other noteworthy schools (University of Southern California, University of Washington and a few others), OSU found itself without a suitor—and without a conference. So, it cobbled together a series of football opponents for 2024, but it lost its star coach and many nationally-ranked athletes because they wanted to go where the money and visibility were. So, after having just completed a $162 million renovation of their football stadium, OSU found itself without a league and without their traditional rivals, though they did play the Oregon Ducks early in the season and suffered a rather humiliating defeat. Apart from that loss, however, the season began well (it often does when you pad your schedule with teams like Cal Poly or Perkins School for the Blind) and they were 4-1 by early mid-season. But then, the bottom fell out. A series of narrow defeats and total collapses brought the Beavers and their fans to the edge of despair.

Which sets the context for THE TAILGATE. I was walking to the game in a Northerly direction along 35th after parking my car at a school near 35th and the Philomath Highway. The usual plan was to walk North along 35th to Washington Street, turn right (East) and then head to 26th, where the open plaza in front of Reser Stadium greets all comers. I so much loved that walk, even in the bracing cold and threatening rain of mid-November. I loved seeing the "layers" of history unfolding before me as I passed by modern buildings of federal agencies and then went by the stately and large early 20th century building on 30th with the word "Poultry" engraved over the entrance, silent testimony to the time when a whole building was devoted to chickens. But along the way, there were horses and other animals grazing on the generous fields less than ½ mile from Reser Stadium, again a testimony to the glorious agricultural history of the place.

What you realize is that when you have a layered approach to history you often recognize the juxtaposition of architectural oddities, and it gets you thinking. So, I escaped in my mental space upon seeing an big, old and decrepit building right next to the modern federal building on Washington Street between 35th and 30th, and my mind started to wander. Why, I asked myself, haven't they torn down that old one? What, actually, is it (or what WAS it)? I looked on a historical map and saw that it had been called the "Manure Shed." Not too many people would embrace that designation today or want to be located near it. Just think if someone from DC was in town wanting to visit the federal building next door. "Where are you?" "Hmm..next to the Manure Shed." Well, I looked at the Manure Shed, and the following "imaginary story" started to take shape. I noted that the Manure Shed extended perhaps sixty or seventy feet North of its inauspicious Washington St. entrance, and it actually shared a parking lot in the rear with Poultry building on 30th. And, *mirabile dictu,* there was a tailgate party going in that very parking lot. Like Moses before the burning bush, I felt I had to turn aside to see this great sight, a tailgate party between the Manure Shed and the historic Poultry building. I decided to approach the party, making sure to keep my distance so that no one would either invite me to join or kick me out. Just at that moment the door burst open from the Manure Shed, and several ladies exited it, with steaming platters of something that I couldn't clearly see. Apparently they were supplying food for the party, though I thought it was a little strange to have the quality foodstuffs coming from the Manure Shed.

Well, people seemed to be oblivious to the source of their food, but were celebrating with each other rather glumly, since the Beavers were coming off of a five game losing streak and their opponent today was ranked in the top 25. Copious drinks seemed to dull their sensibilities. But it also seemed to dull their awareness of what they were eating, because within moments of the women's appearing with the steaming platters from the Manure Shed, people were eating and then beginning to hold their stomachs and vomit. People stood up, beginning to scream in pain, or they fell down on the ground, writhing in unexpected agony. No one seemed to be sure of what was happening, but the torment began to spread as more people consumed the steaming offering from the Shed. Sooner, rather than later, one sage older man got up, walked over to me (since he saw me observing things), identified himself as a professor of veterinary medicine and said laconically, "Shitty season. Everyone should feel it." As I left, I could hear the distant sirens of ambulances. Now the fans were feeling the way the players no doubt felt.

10
Freezer Man

June 24, 2024

AFTER THE PREVIOUS STORY ABOUT "STEAMING" plates of manure, I think I need to retreat to a "colder" topic, and this topic, regarding an acquaintance of mine I can comfortably call "freezer man," fits my need. To set the context: Several mornings a week I walk over to a spacious coffeeshop with ample seating for people engaged in all kinds of activities, from individual to group study, to meeting with clients, to conversations among seniors, and to any kind of meeting where one doesn't want a place as intimate as one's living quarters or as formal as an office. One of the virtues of such a place is that it provides good opportunities for meeting and talking to all kinds of people. Freezer Man, as I call him, is one such person.

I noticed him for the first time about a year ago. His appearance was scruffy but clean, his hair and beard rather unkempt, his clothes loose-fitting, but his manner was courteous and even deferential. He seemed to be more comfortable associating with the more marginal people who hung out at the coffeeshop than with the professional crowd. I learned from the security staff that his name was "Ted" and that he had just gotten out of prison. No wonder I hadn't seen him previously—he was in prison.

Running into people who have spent time in prison or other forms of state confinement--from a few months to several years --is common in my town. The town proudly boasts several prisons and mental health hospitals. If you add to that population the number of their relatives that flock to them to care for them or, more probably, to try to get some of the state benefits that flow their way, the town takes on a social flavor somewhat above, but not strikingly above, the character of those institutions.

Well, Mr. Ted, as I first called him, had been a prisoner. He was now free, but his distinctive saunter and apparently carefree mien betrayed a familiarity with the kind of self-presentation that enabled him to survive in prison. I was interested to learn his crime but I had too much class just to come out and ask him. But I deftly insinuated my way into the good graces of one or two people he associated with at the coffee shop, and I overheard the word "freezer" mentioned a few times. So, with my skill at internet sleuthing, and with the scant clues of first name and "freezer," I was able to discover not only why he only began coming to the coffeeshop about a year ago (he had just been released from prison) but of the crime that sent him there in the first place.

The story is as follows. About eight years ago he, then a man in his mid-50s, was living with his father in a trailer on a road north of town that was only known as the "cutoff road," since its sole mission in life was to get people from the state highway to the federal highway a few miles away. His father was in his 80s, and his health had been declining for several years. Dad managed to eke out a penurious existence on a $2500 a month check from Social Security. Well, as time went on his condition deteriorated yet further. Ted, however, got a brilliant idea. He got himself named as his dad's financial executor so that he had access to his dad's money. He then decided to call his father's medical provider, tell them his father was "fine" and didn't need any further medical care. Finally, he went out and purchased immense supplies of large plastic bags. Then he waited. No one knows exactly when it was, but his dad died fairly soon thereafter. But Ted soon discovered that the checks from Social Security kept coming. This was a dream come true. He decided not to tell anyone about the death. To his two siblings, who lived in opposite sides of the state, he reported that dad was with the other one; to neighbors who noted dad's absence, Ted reported that he had a new girlfriend and they were "traveling."

But Ted had to do something with the body. He couldn't just let it rot. He couldn't also report it to the authorities or there would be a death certificate issued and benefits would stop. This is where the freezer comes in. He stripped his dad naked, covered him with immense amounts of plastic bags and deposited him in a large freezer in the trailer. What could be better? All parties were kept at bay, dad was "frozen," Ted was picking up a monthly check and the rain still came in the Winter. A year passed and Ed's not very finely crafted story began to collapse. One of the siblings had the brilliance to call the other sibling and they compared notes and realized that dad wasn't with either one of them. Ted's faltering attempts to explain this contradiction led them to request some reporters to look into the story. Ted got ample warning that something was "up" when a reporter came to the trailer asking about the whereabouts of dear old dad. Ted said without great emotion that he felt his dad was "fine." But rather than do anything, Ted just waited—and it took the authorities just two more days to raid the trailer and find dear old dad, still frozen in big plastic bags in the freezer.

Ted was hauled away, pleaded guilty to the crime of abusing a corpse and ended up with a five-year sentence that was reduced as time went on because of Ted's exemplary prison behavior. When he got out of prison about a year ago and made it to the coffee shop, he joined a motley collection of professionals, earnest ministerial types and fellow former prisoners. Sometimes it was hard to tell the difference. Everything went somewhat well for Ted until I happened upon him talking to a person in front of the coffeeshop. The person was peddling a huge bicycle and Ted was asking him about it. The fact that Ted had not fully dealt with the psychological fallout of some of his previous crime activity came out when I overheard him say to the bicyclist, "That bike is so huge it has room for a freezer attached to the front." The bicyclist thought nothing of the remark, but I wondered if Ted was suffering from the rare condition known as "RFM" or "Recurrent Freezer Memories."

A month or so later Ted decided to move into the neighborhood of the coffee shop. He, like many ex-cons during and after the Pandemic, learned that finding affordable housing after prison could be a challenge. He had no savings; it was difficult for a man now in his early 60s to find work and, sadly for him, the federal benefits had stopped by now. Yet, he managed to cobble together enough money to get an apartment a few blocks from where I lived. I gulped when I realized this, but I figured that since his crime was directed at a person for a very specific reason, that I had nothing to worry about. Well, as I was walking the neighborhood one day I saw a delivery truck pulled up in front of his apartment building. He was helping two young men unload something into the building. I was close enough to read the markings on the side of the package: a Frigidaire 6.5 cubit foot retro upright unit.

It seemed like Ted still had freezers on the brain, but at least his activity seemed pretty innocent at this juncture. There is no law about being obsessed with freezers just as there is nothing against older people indulging harmless habits of playing old video games. So, I thought nothing of it. Until, as he and I were talking one day, he said he "regretted" that he had to get an apartment here because he wanted really to live with his wife, about 30 minutes away. His wife had dementia and needed care, and her social security payments were just enough for her to pay for her housing and care. He looked at me with a faraway look: "I think I ought to honor the Biblical pattern of a man living with his wife. I will go up next week and see what I can do to get her moved in with me in Salem. I have to work on some financial details, but I am confident I can do it."

I blanched and wondered if he was simply returning to his earlier ways: whether in fact he might be among that rare but dangerous category of "Freezer Recidivist." I thought for a minute that I would contact the ministerial staff of the church that owned the coffee shop, but then I realized that however specialized their ministries were they probably didn't have a "Recovering Freezer Men" support group. Then, I wondered if I should alert the authorities, but I knew that the test in law leading to legal intervention was a clear and present danger test and not simply a vague concern that a third party may have about an unspecified danger. So, I let it go, even when Ted proudly told me a few days ago that his wife was going to be moving back in with him. He said, "We have been apart now for several years, and it has been a chilly time for us. It took me a while to warm up to the idea, but now I am ready." He walked away with his characteristic saunter, and I made sure I began subscribing to the local paper.

11
Tooth Extraction

August 1, 2024

My friend had finally gotten to a place in life of almost complete calm and comfort. His retirement checks appeared regularly and in increasing amounts; his home was paid for; his cars were leased but always in tip-top condition with front seat perfectly elevated so that his butt could effortlessly slip onto the seat from a standing position. His family was scattered in a three-state area but everyone was apparently healthy and well-disposed towards each other. He showed up at the same coffeeshop at 7:04 each morning and ordered the same mocha drink served at 179 degrees. This was after arising at 6:30 a.m. to a perfectly temperature-controlled home. This year they experimented with sleeping at 71 degrees; last year it was 70 degrees. But at 6:31 a.m. the system automatically rose to 75 degrees so that he could be in perfect comfort as he dressed for the day.

He often clothed himself in up to five layers of garments, based on the temperature of the outside air. If it was under 40 degrees, he wore five layers: undershirt, t-shirt, long-sleeved shirt, vest, and outer coat. For every ten to fifteen degrees the mercury climbed, he shed one of the five layers. If there was more than a ten percent chance of rain, he brought two umbrellas: one for the car and one to carry with him when he walked. He once spent an afternoon lining up and then experimenting with fifteen brands of windshield cleaner so that he could discover the one that would most effortlessly and completely wipe out even the slightest imperfection or smudge from the windshield. There was, in short, never a moment of discomfort for him, never a moment where the wind or sun or cold or heat would destabilize him from the perfection of creature comfort.

Thus, it came as a bit of a surprise to him one day when he faced something uncomfortable that he couldn't get rid of by adjusting the temperature or the level of the car seat. A tooth, First Molar number 19 to be exact, began to ache slightly. Or, he thought it began to ache, but he wasn't sure if what he felt was pain, since that sentiment had been so banished from his experience that he didn't properly know what pain was any longer. So, he ignored it, and the feeling went away. But then it returned and he went into full panic mode because there was nothing he could do to get rid of the discomfort. He made an appointment with the dentist who, after X-rays and personal examination, concluded that there likely was an infection in the tooth, and that extraction was the desired method of dealing with this problem.

The man, call him Howard, was nearly apoplectic. Extraction? People die from that, don't they? And if they don't die, they are in excruciating pain. He did a quick online search and discovered that though there were drugs that might get one through the procedure without pain, the pain on days two to five after extraction could be severe. My friend began to visit drug stores with regularity, buying them out of their supplies of over-the-counter pain-relieving drugs, hoping somehow that the discomfort he thought might come his way wouldn't actually engulf him and leave him in a puling puddle of pain.

But ultimately he had no choice. He had to schedule the extraction of the tooth. Just imagining that the tooth was infected and was daily spreading its infection was enough to make him nearly lose his sanity. He imagined that infection was like those little crawling bugs that you see eating the inside of a decaying tree, and he imagined that they were multiplying within him daily, bringing him closer and closer to an ignominious and utterly excruciating death. The dentist tried to alleviate the panic by saying that tooth extraction was relatively routine, but my friend felt that bordered on medical malpractice, and he was getting ready to file a complaint against the dentist until I calmed him down. But I greatly miscalculated my ability to talk him down from the ledge. For example, in my attempt to bring some order to his life I showed him a website which said that the chances of tooth extraction being fatal were very small. But when he saw the words "extraction" and "fatal" in the same sentence, he went into a further tailspin, and just wanted to doctor to prescribe the strongest pain-reliever known to man until the extraction.

Finally, the big day came. Extraction was scheduled for 3:30 p.m. My friend started taking pills at 7:00 a.m., first a steroidal pill and then, a few hours later, several amoxicillin pills. He was only supposed to take two, but figured that four would speed up his comfort level. It didn't, and so when he showed up an hour early for his appointment he was still feeling unprotected and vulnerable as well as increasingly woozy. Sitting in the waiting room was like sitting on burning coals. Every three minutes he popped up to see if the dentist had forgotten him. Indeed, it didn't help that his name was "Howard," since the first words uttered by the receptionist in greeting other patients was "How are you?" which, to my friend, sounded like she was repeatedly calling his name. He began, truth be told, to lose his mind as he jumped up repeatedly because he thought his name was being called.

At length, 3:30 arrived and he was called into the operating theater. He felt that the calm he sensed around him in the staff was a foreboding calm, as if they knew he was going to be toast within minutes, and they were lulling him gently to his death unawares. This heightened his sensibilities still more, until they gave him a shot of something that relaxed him immediately. He didn't fall asleep, but he sunk comfortably into the dental chair, with eyes closed. But he still was on hair-trigger worry alert, and when he opened his eyes to see the dentist's face surrounded by her long hair with a halo glow behind it (from her examination light) he thought he had a vision of the haloed Jesus who was coming to take him home. He reached out his arms and said, "Jesus, I'm yours!" though throughout his life he had never confessed faith in Jesus or any other divine figure.

An hour later, the procedure was complete, and Howard was sent home with a supply of pills. He took a few too many, and then everything hit him very hard at about 7:00 p.m. that night, sending him into a stupor that lasted until the next morning at 6:30. He awoke and wondered at first where he was, but then he saw he was in his own bed, at his own home, and that the temperature was gradually ramping up to 75 degrees. He got up, went to the coffee house at 7:04, texted me and wondered where I was. I showed up shortly thereafter and, knowing his anxieties and fears, gently asked him, "How are you doing? How was it?" "Piece of cake!" was his response, as he returned to playing Wordle.

12
Entitled Women
September 9, 2024

Most of life, for most people, consists simply of muddling through. Sometimes there is a breakthrough or insight or love or some kind of experience that confirms that life is worth living and that it has even vouchsafed some of its precious gifts to us. But often life consists of a series of humdrum experiences or disappointments as one vainly or successfully tries to negotiate the complexities of life.

One of the most confusing things to negotiate is love. Love is both the simplest and most difficult thing of life. The desire to experience and express it, in gentle or more intense ways, is hard-wired into our system and we seek, often unawares, ways to discover it. Thankfully, many people enter into relationships with a spouse that become permanent, and these relationships provide many more benefits than deficits. Without needing to go into details, it provides comfort, security, intimacy, someone with whom to talk and do things, children and, eventually, grandchildren. But also there are tensions, anxieties, conflicts and even hostility over in-laws, money, health, children or the needs of each person. To use poet Wallace Stevens's phrase, even good marriages are, at best, a "blessed rage for order." Yet, sometimes life offers a man an extensive period of singleness, and the challenges and invitations from that life are numerous. I know such a man, Dennis, who has been single nearly a quarter century, and has kindly told me stories of his successful and, truth be told, mostly unsuccessful ways of trying to negotiate the multiform complexities of singleness. Take dating, for example. Dennis is a competent professional, an accountant, able to add numbers and produce clean slates of figures for any organization that retains him. He knows how to tidy up loose financial ends, keep the government away from his clients and, in general, clarify this most confusing areas of managing a company.

Yet it is as if Nature, though smiling on him in certain ways, decided to short-circuit his effectiveness in other areas, making him actually clueless in relational complexities and vulnerable to the most simple schemes practiced on him by more experienced females. As he has been dating, he, the accountant, divides the world of female dating targets into three categories: those beneath him socially; those approximately on the same level; and those who live in some kind of economic or social strata that he can only fantasize about. He has experimented with what you might call Category 1 women (beneath him), but finds in every case that things blow up because there simply isn't enough emotional, intellectual, financial or relational 'glue' to hold it together. They didn't appreciate his deep knowledge of numbers; they don't laugh at his jokes ("What's the difference between an accountant and an actuary. . .?"---that kind of thing—I'll encourage you to imagine the punchline). Even though he managed to take advantage of what they have to offer sexually, he had the vague feeling that this kind of relationship wasn't benefitting him or the woman.

But for some reason he hasn't explored relationships with those of similar economic, social or professional status. Perhaps it is because he has "figured them out" and that he feels they will provide nothing new to him. There will just be conversations about work at the hospital or negotiating the complexities of contracts or the excitement of commonplace movies. It will just be more of the terminal boredom that rankles him deeply in his soul. That, however, is only a suspicion because he hasn't really explored connections with this type of woman.

That leaves the woman who are clearly out of his league. They may be in that position because of superior attainments, economic capabilities, knowledge of the world or beauty. He is a bit chunky and out of shape, and some of the women in this category were former models or are in such tip-top shape that he feels like visiting with them is entering into a museum of physical culture. He feels both a vague sense of excitement at meeting them but also a deep sense of personal inadequacy. Yet, he persists because, despite his training and experience, he believes in magic and he hopes upon hope that something will "click" between him and a woman of this "class," and it will just be happiness from here on out. So, he keeps trying here, too, and usually is disappointed. Sometimes he feels humiliated when she invites some of her "beauty friends" over and they seem to be passing secret codes of damning information about him to each other. But he gets good meals, good views and comfortable settings.

He has also learned a new word or, better said, an old word that now has a special meaning for him. It is "entitlement." He grew up in the era of President Ronald Reagan, who railed against welfare queens and their sense of "entitlement" for needing a few hundred public dollars a month so that they could support their families. He always, therefore, had associated an "entitlement" mentality with poor people who were mooching off the system. But once he had a chance to become immersed in the world of upper-class ladies he realized that what some of them offered, in an unabashed form, was an attitude of entitlement. He was actually shocked at first by the attitudes of more than one of these women, attitudes that tended to belittle and make unfair demands on workers that they hired to maintain their palatial estates both in America and elsewhere. He thought that she must have hired people of limited skills or ne'er do wells until he actually saw them work and concluded they were diligent, capable and loyal workers. So, he wondered at first why these women of high means and cultural standing would act this way towards "lesser people." He kept his mouth shut because the meals they provided for him were delicious, and he got to lounge around infinity pools in the afternoon when the mercury topped 85 degrees.

While he was with these women, he began to notice other peculiarities of them. They were rich, but they hated paying taxes to the government. It seemed as if they were worse than President Reagan's "welfare queens" in many ways, since the latter category openly received only a few hundred dollars a month from the government but the rich women seemed to want to fleece the government of thousands a month—usually in unpaid taxes or hiding income through complex networks of interlocking companies. So, gradually, the food that tasted so delicious in his mouth began to taste not so good. He swallowed his pride, along with the food, and decided that he would "overlook" these examples of what he increasingly saw as "entitlement" in some of these women. It was shocking to him to realize that the word "entitlement" kept recurring in his mind, since he formerly associated this concept only with people at the other end of the economic spectrum. He hadn't yet realized the truism that those who attack others, especially in the public arena, often practice the same things they accuse the others of practicing.

So, like Miniver Cheevy, he thought, and thought, and thought about it. He had identified this "entitlement" attitude in two areas to date: the way that they treated 'lesser' people and the way they tried to 'hide' money that legitimately belonged to someone else. If he got to know them further, he would have discovered that they also specialized in cutting in lines, though usually this was for something very vital in life like access to justice or medical services, but to date he only saw these two characteristics. But something began to make him feel even a bit more uneasy. He had the distinct impression, as time went on, that HE, too, was one of the "help," and that his various skills, which they said they appreciated in him, were simply brought closer to them so that they could be exploited. Then, he thought about it. He had prepared the tax returns, gratis, for both of the women. He had, actually, violated the first principle of accountancy, by not being faithful to the "public," by coming up with somewhat complex schemes to "bury" some of the dramatic income from foreign and domestic rental properties. He discovered, in a word, he was being "used." But, he was also being fed and was enjoying the infinity pool.

Yet Dennis began to feel that his own dignity was now being compromised, even as the entitled women serially told him of his value, his good looks, his intelligence and what he brought to their lives. He began to hate himself inwardly, though he also was skillful at suppressing his self-hatred because of the benefits that came his way. But finally, one day, he snapped. He realized that if he gave them a lecture on their entitlement that it would fall on deaf ears and he would forever be excluded from a world he increasingly wanted no part of. He was, in fact, a bit afraid of them because they might be able to activate their friends to do bad things to him. But he couldn't easily slink away from them, for they would pillory him and question him as to why he was leaving. He felt like he was, in a way, in the Mafia and that raising your hand to say that you wanted to "find your bliss" was a prelude to "finding your grave." So, he began to hate himself yet further, eating more, gaining weight, and generally feeling like the most miserable person on earth. He envied his married friends, and he thought that the finest life on earth would be that of sitting in one's room at night with a pug curled up at one's feet, looking up longingly for affirmation and, of course, food. But he decided to continue the path of self-hatred and keep up with the entitled women, despite knowing that nothing would change and that he soon would be of little more value to them than the dust they threw in the dumpster every day. So, he decided to turn his skills to writing, and authored what turned out to be a twenty-first century classic: "Timely Thoughts on the Dignity of Man."

IV

Two Contrasting Genres—Sermon and Legal Brief

13

The Woman Who Loved Too Much

Sermon Delivered at Westminster Presbyterian Church, Portland, Oregon

March 12, 1989

Note: A NY Times bestseller: *Women who Love Too Much,* by Robin Norwood, appeared in 1985. I was playing off that title, though not reflecting on the content, in this sermon. Yet, the theme of women for whom being in love means being in pain, which is a message of the book, is also not far from my main point below. I preached this sermon while I was Interim Pastor/Head of Staff at Westminster from May 1988-Oct. 1989.

Text: Mark 14:1-9: "It was two days before the Passover and the Festival of Unleavened Bread. The chief priests and the scribes were looking for a way to arrest Jesus by stealth and kill him, for they said, 'Not during the festival, or there may be a riot among the people.' While he was at Bethany in the house of Simon the leper, as he sat at the table, a woman came with an alabaster jar of very costly ointment of nard, and she broke open the jar and poured the ointment on his head. But some were there who said to one another in anger, 'Why was the ointment wasted in this way? For this ointment could have been sold for more than three hundred denarii and the money given to the poor.' And they scolded her. But Jesus said, 'Let her alone; why do you trouble her? She has performed a good service for me. For you always have the poor with you, and you can show kindness to them whenever you wish, but you will not always have me. She has done what she could; she has anointed my body beforehand for its burial. Truly I tell you, wherever the good news is proclaimed in the whole world, what she has done will be told in remembrance of her.'"

Opening Prayer: Lord, teach us what we need to learn, and help us do what we ought to do, through Jesus Christ our Lord, AMEN.

THE STAGE WAS SET FOR THE last chapter of Jesus' life. Within two days he would be dead. Just three days earlier he had entered Jerusalem with great fanfare and celebration. But then, so it seemed, things had gone awry. He alienated the religious leaders by teaching that they were really rejected by God. He alienated the Jerusalem "Chamber of Commerce" by overturning the tables of some card-carrying members who were trying to earn a living by selling and buying within the temple precincts. Finally, he angered a disciple, Judas, through various actions—perhaps including the story read a moment ago. The tide was rapidly turning against him.

The story just read captures some of the intensity of the moment. In the story we have many striking contrasts. There is the contrast between the tumult without, as the religious leaders plot to kill Jesus, and the calm within, as Jesus reclines at table in the house of a friend. There is a contrast between the treachery and hostility of those outside and the pure devotion of one solitary woman inside. Finally, there is the contrast between the violent death through rough handling, which the authorities want, and what you might call the death through tenderness, to which the woman's actions point. Outside all is swirling around; inside there is calm. Outside, in the words of Psalm 46, "the mountains are shaking and the waters roar and foam," while inside, "God is in the midst. She shall not be moved."

Actions are contemplated outside and inside. But it is the characters on the inside who are the focus of the story. Three characters or groups of characters are important—the woman, whose who get angry with her (probably the disciples) and Jesus. The woman is the one who drives the story. It is her initiative which evokes responses from the others.

We know nothing about the woman beyond this story. The Gospel of John tells a similar story, and identifies the woman with Mary, the sister of Lazarus, whom Jesus raised from the dead. This makes sense, since she is the same Mary who sat attentively at Jesus' feet in the Gospel of Luke while her sister Martha was distracted with much serving. But Mark does not identify the woman.

We learn that she is a woman of daring and devotion. She reminds me of the woman in Mark's Gospel who had a hemorrhage for twelve years. That woman heard that Jesus was near, and she broke through a throng around him, thinking to herself, "If I even touch the hem of his garment, I shall be healed." She is daring because she does not let social convention stand in the way of her approach to Jesus. She enters into a house that is not her own. There is no evidence that she has an invitation. She interrupts a person's meal. And, without further ado, she lavishes attention upon a guest and not the host. She is daring because she knows where she must go, she knows the obstacles in her way, and she keeps going.

But the act which she performs also shows her total devotion. She took an alabaster flask—and the best ointment is preserved in alabaster, according to an ancient source—and broke it and poured it over Jesus' head. The contents of the flask were worth more than 300 denarii—more than a year's wages for a worker. Mark is trying to say that she gave a great deal to Jesus, arguably more than any of us would be willing to give at any one time—a year's salary. She is performing an act of pure and total devotion. Perhaps it is even true that the flask and the ointment are like a family heirloom—a precious ointment in a precious container, passed down from mother to daughter, kept in a special place, worth perhaps 300 denarii if sold on the open market but worth far more, perhaps even priceless, to the woman, because of sentimental associations.

So the woman gave herself fully to Jesus. She gave something of extreme value. She abandoned herself to Christ in one heroic and daring act of personal consecration. She didn't care what people said. She had a love and commitment to this Christ and nothing could keep her from giving her all. She loved so much. Perhaps she even loved too much.

But let's freeze the action for a moment. Let's stop the video camera right when the ointment is running down Jesus' garments, while the broken flask is still in the woman's hands. What do we find? We find an uninvited woman who has given of herself in an uninhibited fashion standing in the company of men. And do you know the dynamics of that situation? All of a sudden this bold, daring, loving, giving, uninhibited woman, who loved so much, is placed in a very vulnerable position. When you give yourself completely to another person, you become very vulnerable in the presence of that person. When a student submits a paper on which she has labored diligently and hopefully, she is very vulnerable to every nuance of professorial response. When a new employee is up for review before one of the senior partners, he is in a terribly vulnerable position. When you give of yourself completely—sexually, emotionally, intellectually—you open yourself to some of the deepest and most rewarding experiences of human life, but you also open yourself to rejection and indescribable pain. How does one describe the pain that might come? It is the feeling, no it is more than just the feeling, it is the certain knowledge that no one, yes no one, will ever really understand or feel what I feel. It is the excruciating experience of knowing, knowing so firmly, that in my deepest longings and feelings and loves, I am alone, I have no companion, and in fact, the darkness is my only friend.

So the woman who has loved so much has placed herself in this most vulnerable position. Why do we keep opening ourselves to possibilities of pain? Perhaps because we realize as we grow up, like the woman in the story to loved so much (too much?), that life doesn't really begin until we give ourselves over to something. Freedom and creativity and life only come to those who have abandoned themselves to something bigger than themselves. The goal of life is not to have a great idea but to give yourself to a great idea or great purpose—to abandon yourself, like the woman, to Christ.

So the woman who loved so much is now in a very vulnerable situation. She has exposed herself, not just to Jesus but to a whole group of reclining men. What does the group do when she has exposed herself? How does a group of men respond to a vulnerable woman? They respond by exploiting her, by criticizing her gift, by ridiculing her in the moment of complete abandonment. One of the other Gospels says that it is Jesus' disciples who do this. Instead of receiving her gift for what it is, the men shut her down. Period. And note how they do it. She has just given her most precious possession, the ointment, and lavished it upon the head of Jesus. Their response was this, "Why have you wasted it?" Your supreme effort, the best you have to offer, and thrown right back in your face, even by the disciples of the one you seek to honor! Her life and her soul and her heart was in that ointment. As she poured it out, she was pouring out her soul to Christ. And their response was, 'What a waste.' 'But it represents everything that I have and am—I'm invested in it.' 'Your work is garbage.' Think of the devastation. I'll bet the woman probably made an immediate vow, in silence, maybe through tears, 'That's it! That is the last time I will ever expose myself! That is the last time that I will ever open myself to exploitation! I will close the door of my life against all comers. They will not get to me gain. I will never love again.' Don't you think that thoughts like this raced through her mind?

Why would these men have done such a thing to her? If they were disciples of Jesus, one would hope that they would reflect something of his spirit. I think they do it for two reasons. First, they are men. And I believe that men as a group behave differently than men by themselves. The dynamics of men in a group with a vulnerable woman are fascinating as well as potentially dehumanizing. First, there is the raised eyebrow—'What have we here?' Then one man in the group will chuckle a bit; another will make an offhand comment about the woman's exposed condition. Then it becomes a free-for-all that finally crystallizes in words like the disciples' paternalistic and patronizing words—'You've wasted your money. Nope, we can't help you. You blew it.' Perhaps the men are guarding their own positions of power. They can recline with Jesus; they don't want anyone, much less a woman, breaking into their inner circle and having direct access to Jesus. So they ridicule, because they know that for a woman thus exposed ridicule is a most painful experience.

But there is a second reason they respond the way they do, and this makes the men look a little better. They are disciples of Jesus. Jesus taught them that they needed to give up all to follow him. In fact his precise words are, "Sell what you have, give to the poor, and come follow me." Don't we realize that that is exactly how the disciples are responding? They ask, "Why wasn't this ointment sold, given to the poor?" They have it correct, don't they? According to Jesus' words, they are correctly reciting the requirements for discipleship. They understand discipleship. So here is the dilemma of the men. On the one hand they are so cruel; but, on the other hand, they really do know Jesus' teachings. This is the dilemma of the exposed woman in that and in our society. The men who ridicule are cruel, mean, spiteful beyond measure—but many of those cruel men really do know how things work and really can tell the truth. Though we would like to write the men off because of their meanness, we really cannot.

Then Jesus speaks. He waits for the other people to respond first. He doesn't cut the disciples off. He lets the evil words be spoken. He waits until the men are finished mistreating her. Jesus doesn't keep cruelty from coming into her life or our lives. But he does give methods for handling cruelty when it comes. Then he speaks both to the disciples and the woman. There are two statements of Jesus which we should not miss. First, he says, "Leave her alone. She has done a beautiful thing to me." Literally, it says, "She has done a wonderful thing in me." Second, he says, "She has anointed my body beforehand for burying." This is the only person in the Bible whom Jesus acknowledges has done something wonderful in him. This is the only person in the Gospels whose work Jesus explicitly says will be told as a memorial of her. What really has she done for Jesus?

I think that the woman who loved too much has helped Jesus come to grips with his own death. Oh, Jesus knew that he was going to die. Plots had been hatched for months against him. I think that Jesus knew that people were out to get him and that he might not live much longer. The Rev. Dr. Martin Luther King, Jr had almost an eerie premonition of his own death just a few days before he was gunned down, when he spoke haltingly about the value of longevity. Jesus knew that he was going to die sooner or later, but when the myrrh ran down his collar, it gave off a distinctive odor. Myrrh was used in antiquity to anoint corpses. When the scent of myrrh filled the room, it all became clear for Jesus. Finally he knew he was not just going to die sometime, but he was going to die now. Finaly he knew that it was all coming to a focus now. "This is it! Ride on, ride on in majesty, your last and fiercest strife is nigh." Yes, nigh, now. The thing towards which Jesus' whole life had been pointing, the date with destiny, the grueling, grotesque, gargantuan Golgotha was now just days away.

And all because of the woman. That is my point. By anointing Jesus she became the instrument through which he realized his final destiny. As the scent of the myrrh filled his nostrils, he gave a slight shudder and realized that his time had come. She had done a beautiful thing in him, because through the anointing, Jesus, deep within his soul, put to rest those questions of uncertainty that had probably been dogging him for years. But note that the woman was only able to do this, she was only able to minister to Jesus, because she had kept on loving. Her love drove her to Jesus, her love resulted in her being exposed before the men, her love couldn't keep her from the pain of ridicule. But her love went straight to the heart of Jesus, straight to his inmost being, and it saved him from his uncertainty. Because she loved so much, too much, Jesus was aided in a way that none of the men gathered around could aid him. She loved so much, too much, but she loved herself right into the heart of God.

The inclinations to stop loving, to put a brake on love, to protect ourselves in loving, are very strong. And I'm not saying that one should ignore these inclinations always. But I know also that there was once a woman who gave herself in love to Jesus and ended up helping him more than any other person that ever lived. Keep on loving, for through loving you will save yourself, but you may also, in some mysterious way, save God.

Let us pray. Open our hearts to love with the abandonment of the woman. Through Jesus Christ our Lord, AMEN.

14
The Case of Dayton Leroy Rogers

In contrast to the foregoing, which reflected the pastoral side of my life, is the following legal memo. I went to law school less than a decade after my ministerial work finished, and then made a slight name for myself by publishing a book on the history of capital punishment in Oregon. I wrote the book as a student but published it while a litigation attorney in Portland. About a decade after leaving legal practice I was still sought out to write memos in death penalty cases. The following memo was written when I was retained as an expert witness in the sentencing retrial of the most notorious serial murderer in Oregon history. I wasn't an expert witness because I had "seen the crime"—rather, I had developed an approach to the economics of the death penalty that were of interest to the client's attorney. This memo preceded my testimony at trial. As expected, he was resentenced to death—no memo could have "saved" him--but it does reflect my legal skills at one point in my life. Pastoral and legal skills—skills I affectionately denominated my "kissing butt" and "kicking butt" skills.

To: XXXX
From: William R. Long, M. Div., Ph.D., J. D.
Re: Dayton Leroy Rogers Case Timeline, Probable Execution Date and Costs
Date: September 1, 2015

Introduction

The purpose of this memorandum is twofold: (1) to show the length of time that the case of Dayton Leroy Rogers ("Rogers") will likely take until his execution, if the 2015 Clackamas County jury decides to re-sentence him to death; and (2) to present the most likely scenario for the costs of a death sentence compared to a sentence of life imprisonment without the possibility of parole ("LWOP"). Detailed attention to the Oregon death penalty process yields the fact that the earliest Mr. Rogers can be executed is 2046, more than 59 years after the commission of his crimes, and at least a decade after actuarial calculations for his probable date of death. The likely cost for the prolonged procedure will be four-to-five times the cost of LWOP.

Rogers and the Oregon Death Penalty Process

The voters in Oregon overwhelmingly reinstituted the death penalty in 1984. At that time one of the arguments of the proponents of the death penalty was that execution was a much more efficient and cost-effective method than life imprisonment. Now, more than 30 years after that death penalty has been in effect, Oregon has not executed a single person who has pursued all appeals open to him.[1] Not a single death row inmate is within five years, and probably

[1] Oregon executed two men in 1996 and 1997, after they had given up their appeals after what I below call Step 1, the mandatory and direct appeal of their sentence of death to the Oregon Supreme Court.

ten, of execution today.[2] In the Rogers case, if his process works smoothly, and nothing about his case has been smooth to date, he still has at least 30 years of appeals remaining to him. Since he is 62 years old now, and the life expectancy of a 62 year-old male is 19.9 years, the quickest he can be executed, if all works smoothly, will be about 10 years after his actuarial death.[3]

A. Oregon's 10-Step Death Penalty Process

In my book, *A Tortured History: The Story of Capital Punishment in Oregon* (Eugene, 2001), I presented the 10-step framework of appeals for the Oregon death penalty. This analysis has generally accepted by journalists and other scholars since then. In a nutshell, those ten steps are, after conviction and sentence to death at the County Court level:

1. Affirmation of Conviction on Direct Appeal to the Oregon Supreme Court
2. Denial of Certiorari or (in one case) a hearing before the US Supreme Court
3. Denial of Post-conviction relief in Marion County Circuit Court
4. Affirmation of that denial by the Oregon Court of Appeals
5. Denial of Certiorari or actual hearing of Post-conviction appeal in Or Sup Ct.
6. Denial of Post-conviction appeal by US Supreme Court.

---

2 Phone conversations with Ms. Teresa Hampton, attorney for Mark Pinnell, and Ms. C. Rene'e Manes, who filed the habeas corpus petition in the Clinton Cunningham case. Jeffery Williams' case, the only other case having been at the federal habeas corpus level for almost a decade, still has not been argued at the Federal District Court, according to the attorney who filed the petition on his behalf.

3 The Social Security Administration provides an Actuarial Life Table on its website: http://www.ssa.gov/oact/STATS/table4c6.htm. A 62-year-old man has an actuarial life of 19.9 additional years, meaning that he will live until age 81.9.

7. Denial of Habeas Corpus Petition in US District Court of Oregon
8. Affirmation of that denial by the Ninth Circuit Court of Appeals
9. Denial of Certiorari by the US Supreme Court
10. Denial of Commutation Appeals to Governor of Oregon under state statute.

That is, under my analysis, unless a person is sentenced to death, he doesn't even enter into Step 1. In my book, based on data up until 2000, and realizing that no one had at that time entered beyond Step 4 in the process, I argued that the length of time from commission of crime until execution would take between 20 and 45 years in Oregon. Now, with the hindsight of 14 more years, and knowledge of the length of time of the federal appeals, I would change that to between 30 and 58 years. The Rogers case is a prime example of the system where a man might spend almost his entire adult life, and up to 60 percent of his entire life, pursuing appeals of a death sentence in Oregon.

B. Application to the Rogers Case

Rogers committed the crimes for which he was sentenced to death in 1987. Now, 28 years later, he is still at the "pre-Step 1" level. He faces a fourth sentencing hearing beginning September 2015 in Clackamas County Circuit Court. The rest of this section will show how long the above-mentioned steps for Rogers will likely take, if all works smoothly. Of course, if on any of these steps a court is convinced that yet another hearing is necessary, one should add at least five and, more likely, ten years to the process.

If he is sentenced to death by the end of 2015, a likely, but rather conservative, timeline for the ten steps is as follows:

1. 2020. Briefing, oral arguments and opinion from the O Sup Ct is now taking about 5-6 years after sentence in county

court. The most recent example is the Turnidge case from Marion County. The crimes occurred in 2008, trial and sentence in the county court was handed down in 2010, oral arguments happened in the Oregon Supreme Court in 2015 and an opinion is expected in 2016.

2. 2021. Direct appeals to the US Supreme Court are routinely denied, but it takes almost one calendar year for the briefing and the denial of certiorari.
3. 2028. The post-conviction process in Marion County, during the 1990s, took about 3 or 4 years, but now averages about 6 or 8. Cases that have been completed, took 7 years (Mark Pinnell), and 8 years (Jeffery Williams). Some current cases (Karl Terry) have gone on for 11 years without a hearing. The process is so lengthy because the basis of the relief is inadequate assistance of trial counsel. Upwards of 100 claims of inadequacy are routine, and often the cases are decided over several rounds of briefing.
4. 2031. The three cases that have gone furthest in Oregon so far (Pinnell, Cunningham, Williams) average three to four years between post conviction petition denial and Court of Appeals denial.
5. 2032. The Oregon Supreme Court can deny review, and often does.
6. 2033. The US Supreme Court often denies review at this stage.
7. 2043. When I wrote my 2001 book, no one had entered into the federal process. Under the statute in place at the time, I argued that the process at the US District Court level should take 3 to 5 years. But in the three Oregon cases that have reached that level for any length of time, we have the following: Cunningham entered it in 2004, Williams in 2007 and Pinnell in 2006. To date, none of these cases has been finally decided at by the US District Court. A glimpse into the complexity and delay at the federal level

can be gleaned from two cases. First, the Pinnell case.[4] After his attorneys filed his petition in 2007 (a year after filing notice), the State of Oregon responded, and the first hearing on Pinnell's claims was in 2009. The judge decided to break up claims between procedural default issues and substantive issues, and the former were only dealt with in the 2009 case. The result was partial summary judgment for the state, with dozens of procedural claims still open. The substantive claims haven't yet been briefed. Ms. Hampton informs me that the case still has at least three or four years to go on it. Thus, this case will take 11 or 12 years at a minimum to complete. The case of Clinton Cunningham shows even more the unpredictability that may happen once a case reaches the federal level.[5] After the federal habeas petition was filed in 2005, the proceeding, at an early status conference, was stayed pending the resolution of irregularities in the first post-conviction procedure. The case was remanded to post-conviction, which lasted five years, and then post conviction appeal took another four. But, as a sign that things may be problematic with the Cunningham case, his second post-conviction appeal was argued early in 2014 and the Court of Appeals has, uncharacteristically, not decided the case. Even assuming that the Court of Appeals affirms, Cunningham will not re-enter the federal system until 2017 at the earliest, and then his process will begin again. We might be looking at a process at the Federal District Court for Clinton Cunningham of 15-18 years, from start to finish . Thus, my 2043 date for Rogers, allowing completion of everything in 10 years, is quite conservative.

---

4 Conversation with Ms. Teresa Hampton, Idaho Public Defender and attorney for Mark Pinnell, on August 26. 2015.

5 Conversation with C. Rene'e Manes, August 31, 2015.

8. 2044. No one has reached this level, so we don't know. Most likely 2045 or 2046, but I accept a conservative timeline
9. 2045. Again, a short denial is expected.
10. 2046. Under the statute, the commutation process takes about 9 months, at least.

The sum of all of this is that the most likely scenario for a "quick" execution for Rogers is no earlier than 2046. In 2046 he will be 93 years old. The actuarial "death" of Mr. Rogers is in 2035, 11 years before his "actual" death according to this calculation.

Costs of Rogers Case

Calculation of costs for Oregon death penalty cases is notoriously difficult, and a convincing fiscal analysis has yet to be performed for the cases. Part of the reason is that all the costs are not collected in one place, that prosecutors have been reluctant to come forth with their actual figures in prosecuting cases, and that some of the costs are borne by the federal government (especially in the last stages), while the majority are borne by the state.

If one wanted to look at the Rogers case, one could break it down into retrospective costs and prospective costs, and the following analysis will focus primarily on the latter. Suffice it to say, however, that for the three previous trials and appeals for Rogers, defense costs alone for the three trials and appeals of Rogers before the current (fourth sentencing hearing) have exceeded $1.7 million. The average defense costs of an aggravated murder case just in the past five years in Oregon, when the case was settled short of a death sentence (such as the LWOP that Mr. Rogers proposes) is $344,700.[6] Thus, the actual dollars spent on the various trials and appeals for Mr. Rogers has been five times the amount of the

6 August 27, 2015 Communication from Mr. Paul Levy, General Counsel of the Oregon Public Defense Services.

average aggravated murder trial cost over the past five years in Oregon when such a case was settled for a sentence less than death.

Going forward, the numbers, though speculative, are just as compelling. Had the State of Oregon agreed to a sentence of LWOP for Mr. Rogers, along with his giving up his future appeals, the only costs (other than medical) for the rest of his life would be the daily cost of incarceration. In current dollars, that amount is calculated at $90 per day. [7] For the 20 years estimated, according to the actuarial tables, remaining to him, the cost of incarceration would be $90X365X20 = $657,000.

But when we look at the reality of costs if he still has all his appeals to pursue, the costs are huge. In addition to the $657,000 for the 20 years of incarceration, there are the costs of both prosecution and defense of appeal to the Oregon Supreme Court, briefing to the US Supreme Court, the lengthy Post-conviction process in Marion County, and the several appeals after that. And, we need to include not simply defense costs in this analysis, but the total cost for Rogers. I simply double the amount of defense costs, since accurate data for prosecution costs isn't available. The latest appeal for Rogers, a decade ago, cost $430,000[8]. Any appeal now would be nearly double that amount, and the costs of the appeal for prosecutors would likely be the same. Thus, the costs for Step 1 appeals would be well over $1million and perhaps close to $1.5 million.

Though figures for the rest of the steps are hard to come by, if one assumes $100,000 for defense of the Post-conviction appeal (a conservative amount) and a matching sum for the prosecution, we have $200,000. Briefing and arguing to the Court of Appeals will

---

7 Professor Aliza Kaplan, "Oregon's Death Penalty: The Practical Reality," *Lewis & Clark Law Review* (17), 2013, p. 36 reported that in 2012 the Department of Corrections said that daily inmate cost was $82.40 My figure of $90, then, allows for inflation for the intervening three years.

8 August 27, 2015 Communication from Mr. Paul Levy, General Counsel of the Oregon Public Defense Services.

likely be in excess of $100,000 for each side. We don't know the costs of the federal appeals, but if the length of documents in the Pinnell case is any indication, we have hundreds of thousands of dollars worth of time and work expended by each side.

Thus, though the numbers going forward are speculative, one can say that if Mr. Rogers' plea for LWOP and dropping future appeals is accepted, the costs will be around $657,000. If, however, he is resentenced to death, the costs will be, approximately, $657,000 + $1,300,000 + $200,000 + $200,000 + $400,000 (federal appeals) + miscellaneous briefing or commutation appeals, or, at a minimum $2.8-$3.0 million. It is fully reasonable, therefore, to conclude that the costs to execute Mr. Rogers will be at least four times those of committing him to prison for the rest of his life.

Conclusion

When both the length of time to pursue the steps remaining to Mr. Rogers by law, if he is resentenced to death, and the costs of those steps are considered, the results are clear and stark. The likelihood of putting Mr. Rogers to death before he dies of old age or infirmity is very small and, by pursuing that strategy, we can be assured that the expenses to reach that end will be at least four times those of his prison costs under an LWOP sentence. A larger exercise in judicial futility could scarcely be imagined.

V

Essays of All Sorts

15
The Art of Conversation

[This originally was a Facebook post that garnered readers numbering in the high single digits. An even smaller number voiced their support or approval.]

Most of us spend a lot of time talking. Sometimes we listen, but often we want to communicate something vitally important to us at the moment, and so that becomes our focus. Much has been written about types of conversation or levels of conversation, and I would like to add to that discussion here. A leading theoretical framework, out of UC Davis, maintains that there are three levels of conversation:

1. **Transactional:** Exchange of Information
2. **Positional:** Exchanging power or attempting to persuade
3. **Transformational:** Co-creating new ideas, sharing and discussing

Though I, also, think in terms of threes for this task, and though I use one of these words, I would frame it somewhat differently.

1. **Transactional:** Primary focus is "catching up" or "requesting information" or "transacting business." This level is surprisingly vital to calm and effective functioning in the world. Most of our life seems to be lived in this space but, surprisingly, very few people develop an understanding of how they best can do this kind of conversation. (Now you can see where another book could go ....)
2. **Idea-Oriented Conversation:** Primary focus is on understanding rather than simply exchanging information. Understanding is sought because occasions for confusion or inadequate perception are so vast. This focuses not so much on comments about people or tasks done or to be done as on the universe out of which these people or tasks emerge. Whereas the first focuses on clarity and accurate information, here the interest is in drawing on a variety of sources to try to understand our lives and current moment. Some questions we try to answer are: What am I trying to do? What resources am I drawing upon to do this? What level of understanding is mine at present? How can I improve/develop that? How can I understand your joy/grief/goals/challenges/culture? We need to develop a language of this kind of conversation as well as the skills needed to open up this kind of conversation. Whereas nearly all people are capable of engaging in Transactional Talk, a much smaller number can talk ideas, about their own or others' lives.
3. **Full-Engagement:** This kind of conversation is not simply with people, but can involve prayer, meditation, interaction with classic or sacred texts, focus on life- transforming ideas and their articulation, attempts to put words on the ineffable. Often when you have these conversations, you lose a sense of time; you become oblivious to your surroundings; you arise with a sense that you have engaged in a task utterly human but, in some ways, fully beyond the human. Few people have these conversations with regularity.

Awareness of our level of conversational engagement helps provide a sense of confidence and serenity in life. Good luck in going deeper in your conversations.

16

My Talent Tree

September 19, 2024

BEGINNING ABOUT SIXTEEN MONTHS AGO, I decided to try to present my skills or talents pictorially. I felt it was salutary for me to recognize at my age what I felt I brought to this life and, in some instances, how that "something" showed itself. I think I waited so long to do this because of a vague and distant Puritan-inspired thought that it wasn't right or useful or, negatively said, it was actually sinful, to spend this kind time thinking of oneself. Thinking of self leads to self-congratulation, to vaunting the self, to pride and then to an epic fall that one usually just reads about in others.

But the lure of task didn't let me go and, as time went by, it not only became more insistent but the emerging picture became more detailed and refined. Finally, in August 2023 I drew my first diagram of my talents or skills in life. I call it today my "Talent Tree," because I depict these skills as if growing like a tree, rooted deeply, and then spreading out to a rich canopy. I then fill out various sections of the tree with a particular talent. I supplemented this first activity with two others: a) whether this talent was something that just "existed" and could be called on whenever I wanted or was something I needed to "work on" (I used the abbreviations

"W" and "N"—"work on" or "not work on"); and b) what level of accomplishment I felt I had in each talent area, from "I" ("incompetent") to "C" ("competent") to "S" ("skilled") to "E" ("expert") to "U" ("unparalleled").

I listed about a dozen of these talents at first, even before I developed the concept of a "talent tree." Then, I split up some of the talents into two and "found" another, so that my August 2023 diagram had fifteen. Finally, I stand today surveying a broad and spreading tree with seventeen talents. At this writing, they are depicted as follows: six talents "in the roots" (representing, I suppose, my most basic or fundamental talents); then three on each side of the canopy, and five at the middle and top of the canopy. Let's review them, one at a time.

1. **Generative Intellect.** This is the most basic and fundamental talent motivating me. In a word, my mind is a fountainhead of ideas. The ideas are derived from a lifetime of study, observation, linguistic awareness and personal interaction. It is manifested in conversations with people where, usually midway in the conversation, I think, "here is a book" or "here is an essay" that person could write to capture what s/he is saying. I then would proceed to "outline the book" in my mind before the end of the conversation. If the person seems open to my thinking, I actually share with them what I am thinking. This isn't something I set out to do; it simply happens that as a person is speaking I can "capture" not simply the flow of thought but also can think of an organizational principle to present that thought. I do this effortlessly ("N"), and I think my talent at this is either at the expert ("E") or unparalleled ("U") level.
2. **Languages.** This is also embedded deeply in the root system of the tree, resting gently on the "generative intellect." This one captures all kinds of things with languages: basic learning, sacred text mastery, memorization, writing,

speaking, vocabulary building. Many of my languages are not studied in order to converse in them; they are ancient and perhaps are primarily important because they capture sacred thoughts or the poetic imagination. I don't set a goal of "mastery" of these more than a dozen languages but rather of "building" knowledge every day in several of them. I often translate works from these languages into English. In a word, I seek deep knowledge of the several classical languages in which sacred texts of about 90% of the world's people are written, and several modern languages. But I have to work at this daily. I have identified 34 languages with which I want more than a passing acquaintance in life, and I work on several of them daily, as time permits. Because I know how much more I need to attain, I characterize my talent level as "S" ("skilled") and that I have to "W" ("work") at it.

3. **English language.** Starting at age 52, I participated in national senior spelling bees. I did this for about six years before the lure of studying many Eastern languages took me away from this task. But in those six years I not only did well in national competitions (finishing 2nd twice and 3rd once), but I began to develop both a vast list of useful and elevated English words, and began to write "better than OED" definitions of some of them. My list now exceeds 34,000 words. Of course one can debate what an English word actually is, and whether proper nouns ought to be included, but this task is ongoing and leads me on the most extensive, arcane, but useful intellectual journeys. I think I am an expert ("E") but I have to work ("W") on it.
4. **Memory.** Memory is one of our most precious gifts. It connects us to the past and to others; it gives us a rich store of images on which we can call. It also declines, inevitably, with age. The lapses or memory failings can often be in rather insignificant areas (e.g., "Who was the guy who

acted in XXXX in 1993?"), even though the basic memory system may be intact. Memory is a profoundly theological concept, too, as both Christianity and Judaism, rooted in the Biblical tradition, are based on the idea of a remembered past ("Remember you were slaves in Egypt" or "This do in remembrance of me"). For some reason, mine is not only largely intact but when combined with a longish life, gives me a kind of depth that I think is really useful. This skill is "U" ("unparalleled") and is a "N" ("don't have to work at")—even though I spend time at lot of time memorizing things in multiple languages.

5. **History.** This may sound imprecise and, of course, includes almost anything in life. I sometimes joke that I became a professor of history in early mid-career, after three or four other ventures, so that I would get "credit" for every book I read. But when you combine memory with a basic commitment to historical investigation—by looking at life as one huge layered archaeological "dig"--then one has all the tools to internalize vast amounts of extremely useful knowledge. One way I combine memory and history, a very practical way, is to learn birth and death dates of people when I learn their names. "Martin Luther, 1483-1546." No one else does this, but when you do it for hundreds of people, you not only will be ready to "place" almost every movement and person in historical context but will convince (or fool) people into thinking you know much more than you do! I waver between "S" and "E" here, but I definitely have to "W" at it.
6. **Textual Interpretation.** I broke this out from textual explication, number 13, because the latter skill includes ability to explain other things beyond texts, but here I just want to focus on the ability to interpret something written that is in front of me. Through training and inclination, through patience with languages and knowledge of the

authorial process, I usually am very good at interpreting or gleaning precise meaning where it can be gleaned from a text. This often leads to seeing multiple possible interpretations of texts because of the plasticity of language, and thus it isn't a skill often welcomed by those who just want "the TRUTH," but it is what I have. I would say that my knowledge is "U" and that I don't have to work at it ("N").

Starting with number 7, I move up the tree to what you might call auxiliary interests or skills. Numbers 7-9 are areas of mastery while 10-12 are ways to consider and organize knowledge.

7. **Poetry.** I have now written two books of poetry, though the second has yet to be published. I am an eager reader of poetry in multiple languages and have discovered that in some (unlike most English poems), poetry is actually easier to read than prose. Learning how to express meaning in fewer words is my goal (you can stop laughing now), and poetry enables that. But I am merely "competent" ("C") in poetry and have to work ("W") at it.
8. **Numbers.** I grew up in a numbers-oriented family. We calculated distance, miles per hour, learned to multiply double digits in our head by age five. My dad was a math major in college and was constantly challenging us to do mental math problems. I am surrounded by accountants in life—dad, two brothers, my son—and the numbers skill has also fallen to me with the result that I can instantly calculate things and also recall numbers with precision. It surprised me when I was a law professor to discover that my students couldn't do that (I used to give them number problems in my Article 2 Sales class and would laugh to myself as they stumbled. Bad prof!). I think I am skilled ("S") here but I don't need to work at it ("N").
9. **Maps.** A friend of mine challenged me a few years ago to "put my life's goals in 20 words or fewer." I don't know

why I rose (or lowered myself) to the challenge, but I said, almost immediately, "To know all the words in multiple languages and to know where all the roads go." And, I concluded, "I still have four words." He thought, with my penchant for metaphor, that I was speaking metaphorically about "roads" and he wondered if this meant I was focusing on different "roads" of knowledge, but I assured him that one of the most pleasurable activities in life for me is learning road names and driving down those roads to see what there was along the way and what was at the end of the road. In preparation for my 50th high school reunion in Connecticut, for example, I memorized 114 road names of my old town—and of where they went. Strange. Really strange. But I would say I am only "skilled" ("S") at this and have to work ("W") at it. Contour and climate maps, for example, aren't interesting to me. . .

10. **Three Talents of Organizing Knowledge.** Now I move to the other side of the tree to emphasize three talents of organizing knowledge. Talent # 10 is Questioning/Listening. I learned how to be a good questioner long before I became a professor of religion and humanities at age 30. I learned the difference between a question that opens the hearers and one that closes off the hearers. But the key to being a good questioner was being a good listener, to hear every nuance of what a person is saying, however ridiculous at times. I therefore "trusted" the process of communication, and decided that one of the most valuable things in life was to practice good listening and questioning. I am really good at this. Unparalleled ("U") and I don't need to work at it ("N").
11. **Reframing.** "Reframing" is a word de jour. Everyone is reframing things. This means that you are trying to see things from a new perspective or angle. I take data, see how it is traditionally or "normally" explained, try that

explanation on for size for a while and then, inevitably, end up "reframing" it. In order to reframe well, one needs a rather vast store of knowledge that can easily be recalled. Major scholarly developments happen because people learn how to "reframe" things. Think of Peter Brown's work in "inventing" the field of late antiquity. He successfully "reframed" the "Fall" of the Roman Empire, which had dominated our thinking since at least Gibbon. My knowledge here is also Unparalleled ("U") and is done effortlessly ("N").

12. **Conceptualization.** This can seem the same or very close to 11, but differs in that it emphasizes not the process of reformulation but of formulation in the first instance. That is, when you come upon a problem or issue in history or life, you generally put words on it to describe it. These words are selected because they somehow "fit" what is before you. But our language is heavily indebted to metaphorical thinking, to "picture-making," and the concepts, therefore, are often rather "squishy." Because metaphor is the neighborhood where I live (I sometimes joke that I was brought up near "Synecdoche, New York"), I generally have my storehouse full of other ways to capture what is in front of us. These "other ways" are not simply re-conceptualizations but are ways of describing a phenomenon more fully than when originally presented. This also is a skill I possess almost uniquely ("U") and on which I don't really need to work ("N").

The remaining five talents are the center or crest of the canopy, but I am not sure why they are there. Perhaps they are there because they belong somewhere on the tree but I am not sure where precisely to place them.

13. **Explication of Texts.** I broke this out from 6 above when I realized that the skill of being able to divine meaning is different from the ability to explain the meaning. Some people, actually, are very good at limning meaning from

texts but are unskilled in presenting what they know. But this skill suggests that I spend a lot of time, and want to emphasize, my skill at "splaining" things. This can be of all kinds of things, from a newspaper article to a sacred text. I would say I am an "expert" ("E") at this but that it comes effortlessly ("N").

14. **Clarity.** This is closely related to the preceding but I think is a separate skill. It not only suggests that I know HOW to explain texts but that my explanation of things is often so clear as to be stunning. Clarity, though, is a concept stretching far beyond explanation of texts, but is a way of trying to capture the movements of the heart, or whatever someone wants explained. One of my Billphorisms, coined nearly twenty-years ago, lamented my possession of this skill: "I suffer from the disease of terminal clarity." I still suffer from it. It is unparalleled ("U") and effortless ("N").
15. **Writing.** I have never stopped writing since my then mother-in-law gifted me with a blank book for Christmas in 1980. Of course, I wrote a lot before then but most of it was "required" writing, even though I still have copious essays I wrote from the mid 1970s to give "guidance" to my Bible study group on the meaning of texts. But the extent of my writing now extends far more than 300 volumes of 40,000 words each. I may be one of the more prolific authors in the English language today now that Jacob Neusner has died. Not all of this is valuable writing; it really can't be. Most of it, even if it was published, would be ignored. But it is there. And, I can easily come up with and write an attractive essay on many subjects very quickly. I think I am "only" an expert ("E") writer because I am no Dostoevsky in literary quality, and it does require work ("W").
16. **Getting Beyond the Façade.** This is often built upon my ability to listen and question, but these skills are often combined with an ability to call on rare but precise bits

of knowledge that relate to the person with whom I am dealing. It results in the ability to get beyond the outer barrier or the castle wall that keeps the riff-raff out of our lives, and allows me access to the center of a person's identity. I can't do this with everyone, nor am I interested in so doing. But by a few deft questions I often can do so. One person has equated it to that kind of insect that stands over its prey, holds it down, and then sucks the life out of it. Surely not complimentary here, but they meant it in a complimentary way. This comes rather effortlessly ("N") and I am probably an expert ("E") at it. I don't use it often; really no need to. I look at it as a kind of martial art, which a skilled artist rarely needs to demonstrate [I have multiple examples of how this has worked to yield understanding, though I won't relate them here].

17. **Humor.** I hesitated for a long time to include this last skill, but then I realized how valuable it was. I use it all the time, often to lower the emotional temperature of an encounter, and often to tell the other person that I am "with them." I think I am an expert ("E") at this, and I really don't need to work at it very much "(N").

These seventeen skills make up my "skill tree." I offer these to the world, and am grateful to that same world, and its Creator, for entrusting them to me. I hope I have been worthy of this entrustment.

17
Reflections on Decline
August 12, 2024

ONE OF THE IRONIES OF HUMAN life is that occasions that are supposed to give a clear and even unequivocal message, either positive or negative, often unintentionally bring in their wake the opposite message. A case in point is a family wedding. Everyone is supposed to be celebrating the nuptials of the happy couple, but on more than one occasion such a celebration has led to conflict which created an unbridgeable chasm between family members. On the other hand, a memorial service for a child or young person is often draped in the most morbid and gruesome emotional crepe but has been the occasion at times for people to create positive memories and even connect in lifetime relationships.

So it happened on Saturday, August 10, when the Oregon Senior Games, a celebration of the seemingly boundless energy and athletic prowess of older citizens, became for me the occasion of prying open the delicate subject of bodily and mental decline. More specifically, it opened up my own "decline" as a 72 year-old male. I say it is a "delicate" subject, because there are few things that bother a 72 year-old athlete more than the thought that his performance is irreversibly tapering off.

But "decline" in one's seventies isn't just limited to fears of athletic diminution. Many beautiful women, now in their 70s, fear that fading physical attraction is a sign that she may be superannuated and even a bit ugly; many accomplished men, now in their 70s, fear that the complexity of new concepts, language and technology not only makes them obsolete but even somewhat offensive to much less accomplished people a generation younger than they.

So there we were, running and throwing our hearts out in Corvallis, Oregon at the same time that Paris Olympians were throwing objects three times as far or running four times as fast. Yet it wasn't simply the contrast between the speed or strength of these two sets of athletes that was striking; what tended to gnaw at me was the sense that the pattern or direction of my own accomplishment was diminishing by the year. What was a shot put of 8.4 meters one year became 8.3 the next and then, surprisingly, about 7.8 this year. It was as if the numbers over time became etched in my consciousness, a silent witness and jeering spectator saying that the end, if not already here, was near.

In the middle of these not-so-edifying musings I looked up and saw two friends who had decided to show up and cheer me on. They are an accomplished medical couple, Thomas and Mary, whom I met by chance about seven months ago on an airport shuttle while we were off to our adventures to different parts of the country. Within three minutes of that first encounter we knew we wanted to see each other again, and they have graciously extended repeated invitations to me to join them for dinner and conversation. On this August 10 they were there in the unintended role of personal counselors, though our conversational ease mostly tended to cover my own growing dis-ease with my performance and worry about "decline."

I broached the issue gently in between throws, and they both were supportive, understanding and insightful in response. Thomas was a great champion of doing things that, if not "fun," brought a kind of benefit to life, while Mary, as befitting a doctor who wanted to define a problem with a global term, talked knowingly about "managing decline." I thanked them both, went back to my throwing, and then finished the day. Their words, and my own thoughts, continued to swim about in my mind as I tried to come up with a way of recognizing and giving decline its due, to speak in the language of Greek philosophy, while at the same time embracing the promise and joy of competition and physical accomplishment at my age. I then retreated to my son's home in town, where we continued the discussion in the context of his recently completed half-marathon. He was kind enough to admit that he didn't really understand the concept of decline I was talking about, though he readily admitted, as a 37 year-old male, that he felt nothing like he did at 32.

Yet, I was looking for a system or a kind of conceptual explanation for what I felt deeply within, and so far I was coming up with a blank. So, I did what I usually do when I come up with a blank—I retreated to an earlier iteration of myself as preacher and decided to come up with a "three-point sermon" on decline. Ah, that started me thinking, and so the first point I decided upon was "Acknowledgment" or "Recognition." Yes, of course, that is always the first point. Be willing to recognize your true condition in life. Don't be in denial; don't try to ignore the question. Even Alcoholics Anonymous says it. Face it and recognize that the issue of decline is real. I felt a sudden surge of satisfaction as I came to this conclusion, not because I had identified one out of three points but because I sensed that I was on a path of personal honesty, and that honesty can only be a good thing.

Thus I would "acknowledge" the fact of decline. Of course, this left all kinds of questions unanswered, such as whether physical and mental decline are partners, whether there are surges of energy once decline has set in, whether there are other activities one can do, like hiring a trainer, who will be able to stave off its more obvious or threatening aspects. But, I embraced the first point: I now have clear evidence of my physical decline. Period. No tears (yet). No complaints (yet). No ill feelings. Just realize that it is as true and as real as was my budding sexuality sixty years ago.

But then I thought further. Acknowledgment of decline isn't the end of the story. Just as Mary suggested the word "managing" decline, I thought of a way to try to see decline as "empowering." Of course, this fits into my theory of irony presented in the first paragraph, but it may also have some truth to it. By acknowledging the fact of decline, I am in a better position, I felt, to draw a kind of positive "lesson" from it. Not only does it put me into common company with millions of other people, but it may be the avenue for me to raise other questions that would have not been raised had I denied the decline. For example, I could see that a robust recognition of physical decline might lead me into other activities (though I hope not pickleball!) that might have their own life and joy to them. I know of a man, for example, who became limited in mobility in his early 80s and decided to take up wood carving, a very technical exercise requiring loads of focused patience. Now, fifteen years later, he is a master carver. Had he looked at his limitations in movement as a death sentence, he never would have discovered this new dimension of living.

I had two points, and I felt gratified. I would acknowledge the physical decline, but I would also leave the issue of mental decline for another day. I might not exactly embrace this decline but I would certainly recognize it, acknowledge it, and say that it is my new reality. I am a person in physical decline, however gradual that decline is. Then, I would seek ways to take this reality and pursue creative outlets that may or may not build on my previous commitments. I would try to look at shot-putting not as the only skill that can be developed but perhaps as a kind of gateway or welcome sign to explore some of the vast diversity of human life.

I was beginning to feel a bit elated, then, as I arrived back home to a late meal and a refreshing shower. But then something continued to gnaw at me. I could acknowledge the reality of decline. I could also see it as a channel of further growth. But something was missing. At first I thought that the thing missing was only that I had betrayed my Protestant pastor sensibility by just having a two-point rather than a three-point sermon, but then I saw that the thing that was missing was actually an idea or a third legitimate point. And, then it came to me. I needed to acknowledge the grief that decline brings. One might recognize decline and give it its due, but what decline really means is that certain things, even important things to my personal identity, are lost, irretrievably so. And when I framed it that way for myself, I began to feel a sense of overwhelming loss and grief.

I remembered that shot-putting was the only activity that generated two poems in my life, written by me at age fifteen when just taking it up and at age seventy when rediscovering it. But it hit me now that these poems may now very well be obsolete. Gone now were the emotions, the memories, the feeling of excitement at participation. All that was left in my emotional self was a sort of empty chasm, a windswept and arid plain, a scorching desert where life had once been. But the worst part about it was there seemingly was nothing to replace it. So, that was the deepest sense I recall feeling as I was home by myself that Saturday night.

I honestly, and not really grudgingly, admitted the reality of physical decline. I embraced and welcomed the ways that this "decline" might be the avenue for new discoveries and new pathways for the future. But now, as the warm water of the shower coursed over my body, I also let the grief of inexorable loss wash over me. All those feelings are there from the little activity of throwing an 8 pound 8 ounce ball, from the conversations with my friends and my son, from personal reflection. Then, finally, I realized today, two days after the event, that all three ideas are still in my mind, and they seem to be raising their hands like impatient students looking for my acknowledgment. I just hope that I have the strength, grace and courage to embrace them all, but somehow be able to honor more the creative future than the numbing grief. Time will tell.

18
A Love Poem

IN THE PREVIOUS ESSAY I TALK about writing two poems about shot-putting, one as a youth and one more recently. The following is my poem written in 2023, shortly before the Senior Games of that year took place. It will appear in my upcoming book on love poems also.

Love for What??—Shot Putting (March 10, 2023)

If God thought seniors should put the shot
He doubtless would not have to think a lot
Just give us arms and legs so strong
That work-out and recovery would not be long

He simply could have decreed
That all the strength and gifts we need
Would easily have been provided
Whether independent or closely guided

And we would certainly grateful be
Having lived so long we know how to see

When external sources give us presents
To receive them with thanks, oh so pleasant

But though we long for bodies sleek
For nimble feet and appearance chic
For supple arms and bulging legs
For all these things we must just beg

Though our wishes are for strength
For form that zings, for throws of length
We cannot tell the legs to move
The knees, the ankles, the hips improve

We can imagine such a throw
That makes our few admirers glow
But it must remain a fitful dream
A yearning, longing not in the genes

For, you see, that though we long
For limbs of power, bodies strong
Our best effort and longest throw
Is far surpassed by teenage show

We are, in fact, a pitiable sort
Evoking laughter, long and short
Making the dictionary incomplete
When it defines clumsy feet

Yet. . .yet. . .I am by it entranced
Returning daily to the dance
Of throwing, lifting, walking sure
Of hired trainer providing more

I am entranced because it evokes. . .
(And what I say is not a joke)
It strums the mystic memory chords
Of long ago engaged not bored

It calls me to another place
Whose odors, green grass, massive space
Fills me with the hope of youth
Makes me long for those years' truth

Brings many people to my mind
Who were so fresh when in their prime
But most now gone, a memory only
Sometimes making me sad and lonely

But even more they bring me strength
Whispering, telling me at length
That what I do would make them proud
That striving at 70 is still allowed

And so as I survey the field
Planning, thinking what it may yield
I am not present in our day
But really am very far away.

19
Piece for Political Scripture

Written in July 2024; Published 9/9/2024

A long-time friend of mine suggested that I might be interested in writing for this left-leaning political/religious blog. The assignment gave me a chance to rekindle my exegetical and homiletical skills more than a generation after I had left paid employment in a church or teaching religion. My text was taken from Proverbs 1.

The Biblical presentation of Wisdom in the Book of Proverbs and elsewhere is both alluring and confusing. It is alluring because it suggests that if we truly understood and appropriated the contours of this divine gift, we would have mastered a key aspect of faithful living. But it is confusing because its cry to us often is drowned out by the cacophony of competing cries which flood the marketplaces of our lives. This week's lectionary reading/The passage for today recognizes both Wisdoms and recognizes their alluring and confusing character. Three things to note about wisdom in this passage are its *easy accessibility;* the *human tendency to ignore it*; and, finally, the *reward for listening to it.* Wisdom is especially helpful to us today when we consider its value in thinking about politics, our approach to personal finance and investments, and history.

A few words, first, about Wisdom in the Book of Proverbs and in this passage. Proverbs, like no other book of the Bible, captures the tension between the secular and sacred understanding of the idea of Wisdom. On the one hand Wisdom is seen as a divine gift, and the quest for it begins with the fear of the Lord (Prov. 1:7). But, on the other hand, Wisdom can be understood as the distilled and often lapidary exposition of principles gleaned from the experience of living in the world. The tension between its divine origin but human discovery can stimulate us to make it our own. In this passage Wisdom is personified, and it calls out in the public squares with its message.

The first thing to notice is Wisdom's *easy accessibility*. The Hebrew text of 1:20 captures this perfectly by placing the word that literally means "wide open space" (*rehovot*) as the fourth of seven words in the verse. Wisdom, literally, resides in the public square, and that public square is right in the middle of the verse. It is therefore accessible to all, calling to all, beckoning to each one of us to listen to it. Interestingly, the Hebrew word for Wisdom is feminine, giving us the impression of a higher-pitched lilt calling us over the words of the crowd. Maybe that is why people have ignored it historically and today. People often associate wisdom with a lower vocal register. But the Scriptures teach us it is the *Chokmoth* (literally "feminine wisdoms," as it appears in the feminine plural) which beckon/s.

Yet people *don't hear*. And that is our second point. The author of Proverbs talks about various groups on whom the voice of Wisdom falls. The passage is vaguely reminiscent of Jesus' parable of the sower (e.g., Mark 4), where the word of Jesus falls on various kinds of soil. Here the word of Wisdom falls on various kinds of people: the simple, the scoffer, the fool. This isn't an exhaustive list, as can be seen by the fact that some people actually will respond faithfully to the call of Wisdom. Nevertheless, our author spends several verses talking about how Wisdom's call is rejected and what the judgment on those who reject it will be.

But not all people fit into the Biblical categories of fool, scoffer and simple, even though we can think of ample occasions in our own lives where those titles would capture us perfectly. The final verse of the song/our text, verse 33, gives us *hope*: "but those who listen to me will be secure and will live at ease without dread of disaster." (1:33). The reward for listening to wisdom will be, in the words just quoted, *security* and *ease*. The word rendered "security" is actually a much richer word in Hebrew than captured in our translation. It is the word *betach,* and it originates in the field of "trusting." Those who listen to wisdom live not necessarily with security but with trust as the organizing principle of life. That one word deserves fuller exposition, but suffice it to say that it takes us into the realm of authentic and intelligent engagement with life, rather than just feeling safe.

Engaging Life

And, once we are in the realm of what I call intelligent engagement with life, we are invited by the text to see the variety of ways that life can profitably be engaged or encountered today. I mentioned three above, though the heart of my point here is our political engagement. Let's begin with that point. We live in a time when the most highly-charged, contrary and harmful things are being said in the public square. On other occasions I have written about what I call the "intensification of language" in many fields in our day, and this is evident nowhere more than in our political arena. Words such as "striking" or "shocking" or "bombshell revelation" or "revolution" or other such type of inflammatory language fill our oral and written spaces. In the midst of this, the Scripture tells us that Wisdom is calling. It is a woman's voice, a voice that tells us to turn to her, to turn to finely honed and calibrated principles of living as the basis of life rather than the language of screeching panic. In fact, beginning in Proverbs 2, the Scriptures begin to lay out those principles, beginning in familial relationships, that lead to good living.

We not only need finely honed words of wisdom in our political arena today; we also need something that often isn't broached in "polite conversation": investing money. We have money; some of us manage it better than others. It can be a gift or a curse. It can be all-consuming or relatively ignored. But I have increasingly found in my writing on intelligent investment that people are at a loss to know how best to act wisely with this treasure in our day. And, to make matters worse, when I listen to what many others are saying "out there," I find the cacophony to heighten rather than lessen lesson the problem. Wisdom can be gleaned from basic principles for intelligent investment of our money.

Finally, I have explored elsewhere how we live in a time where possible wisdom gleaned from historical learning is not simply being lost but obliterated. While the Surgeon General may decry social media as a mental health hazard to users, I would say that social media's most noxious by-product is its tendency to erase the concept that there is anything of value in the universe apart from what is happening RIGHT NOW. All the treasures of our past are in danger of being sucked into the whirlwind of presentism. Memory, a wonderfully rich historical and theological concept, is in danger of being lost or diminished. And the major problem with this is that it diminishes the value of nuance and the use of ambiguity to understand our own and others' lives.

Divine Wisdom calls. It is publicly accessible. We may not recognize the voice because we might not be listening for it. But it is there and beckoning to us. Take time to ask yourself what wise living would look like for you with respect to politics, to investments, to understanding history. The gift of Wisdom is sweet: it bequeaths perspective and understanding and what the Scriptures call *betach,* a refined trust that fully engages life.

20
Darien, Connecticut Essays

I SPENT THE FIRST FIFTEEN YEARS OF my life in Darien CT, a pleasant and affluent Fairfield County suburb of New York City. A while back I joined a Facebook group of Darien residents and decided to share a few unique memories of the place that seemed to evoke more than yawns from some people. I began with an essay about the 1946 Darien High School graduation (my mother's class) because of the unique combination of my great uncle's giving the Invocation and Prof. Roland Bainton of Yale Divinity School giving the graduation address. Response to that essay encouraged me to write briefly about a few experiences in Darien before the family moved to another exclusive community in 1967 (Atherton CA). I put a few of those essays/posts here. First are some thoughts about how I first fell in love with words, my life's passion, in Darien. An essay on a memorable Vice-Principal follows. Then, I write humorously (I hope) about my experience running for student body treasurer in Junior High. These Darien essays conclude with our move to CA in the Summer of 1967.

A. Falling in Love with Words in Darien, Connecticut

1. After writing about my mother's graduation ceremony of 1946 in Darien, I wanted to write another small essay reflecting my gratitude to Darien, where my family lived since the early 1930s, and which I left in 1967. This story describes how I, now a writer, fell in love with words--as a schoolboy in Darien.

Here is the scene. One September day in 1961, when I was in 4th grade at Holmes School, my teacher, Mrs. Mesologites, came to class one day with deep sadness etched on her face. She told us the news. The previous day the plane of the Secretary General of the United Nations, Dag Hammarskjold, had crashed/been shot down over Africa, and he and others died. Mrs. Mesologites said, and I recall her voice, that she deeply "lamented" his death.

The only problem was that, at 9 years of age, I didn't know what "lament" meant. So, at a class break, I went over to the well-stocked bookshelf, took down the student edition of our Thorndike Barnhart dictionary, and looked up "lament."

It said, in typical brevity: "mourn."

Only problem, I didn't know what "mourn" meant. Look it up.

It said: "grieve." Didn't know what "grieve" meant. Look it up.

It said: "lament." Oops.

But then a strange thing happened in my mind. Rather than being frustrated that I was in an endless loop of confusion, I became suddenly overjoyed, as if by knowing three new words I could unlock the secret of the universe. That lesson, thanks to the availability of dictionaries and a little curiosity, stimulated my quest for multiple language mastery over the years---thanks to Mrs. Mesologites, who "lamented" Dag's death.

2. This post follows up on a previous one where I described how I, now a writer, fell in love with words in Mrs. Mesologites' fourth grade Holmes School class in 1961. In this brief essay I will describe how my love of words backfired a bit in eighth grade.

   Let me set the context. In seventh grade (1964), I began my adventure with Spanish at Middlesex Junior High. This may have been the first year that the school district offered that language, and they selected a wonderful teacher for it, Miss McGoldrick. Our class consisted of many of my guy friends, such as Steve Cary and Hal Cherry. We also had Pedro Castillo in the class, a native Spanish speaker fairly recently arrived from Cuba, who would feed us answers when Miss McGoldrick wasn't looking. Great class.

   My experience in eighth grade Spanish wasn't as positive. I reverted to some of my bad behavior of earlier years and the teacher, Miss Bielen, occasionally had to throw me out of class. On one occasion she sent me to the office, which meant I had to go see Roger Luce, who will be the subject of my next post. But she also sent me with a note detailing my offense. I became, as it were, the unwitting messenger of my own demise.

   I remember the message clearly to this day, because it only had two words on it: "Chronic Insubordination." I read and re-read the message, but I had no idea what it meant. So, because I already had a love for words, I decided to take a detour to the library and look up what "Chronic Insubordination" meant. First, "Chronic," I learned, meant "persisting for a long time." And "Insubordination" meant "a defiance of authority" or "refusal to follow orders."

   Before going to see Mr. Luce, I stopped and paused for a moment. "This means," I thought, "that I defy authority on a regular basis." I also remember thinking, "Boy THAT hits the nail right on the head!" I was smiling when I gave the note to Mr. Luce, not because I was being further insubordinate, but because I had two more words that I knew, and I knew also how right they were about me in eighth grade.

B. Remembering Roger Luce (1920-2002)

In a previous post I described how my adventure with words in Darien was enhanced in an ironic way at Middlesex Junior High during eighth grade (1965-66), when I learned what "chronic insubordination" meant. But what I only hinted at in that post was that the person to whom I was sent at Middlesex for that offense and the subsequent administration of discipline was the Vice-Principal, Roger Luce. This post will not only describe my experience with Roger Luce at that time but will mention what I know about his life now, nearly sixty years later. I was stunned, to say the least, by my recent learning.

THEN: Miss Bielen, my Spanish teacher, sent me to Mr. Luce because of my "chronic insubordination." Someone here may know the precise years of his service in Darien, but I knew he was a large presence at Middlesex in those years. I still remember him, nattily attired, strutting through the halls, with regal or even imperious bearing, and seemingly joyfully handing out punishments to students who had broken real or imaginary rules. He told me that for my insubordination he was going to give me some "demerits." I didn't know what that word meant either, but my parents had trained me to thank people who gave me things, and so I duly thanked him, only to learn that this meant that one of the most coveted positions for the ninth grade year for boys, being a school monitor (which basically meant you could harass seventh graders as you told them to walk around you in the hall) was denied me. Others have mentioned that this form of discipline, where my alleged offense wasn't even investigated before punishment was dished out, wouldn't "fly" today, but it was the law of the land then. In any case, for the next fifty years, if anyone mentioned the name "Roger Luce" to me, this experience, and his decision to deny me the position of "monitor," would have come back to me.

NOW: But as I was thinking of Darien days and doing some sleuthing on memories, I learned that even though Roger Luce spent many years in Darien, his mind and heart were really elsewhere. He was a Mainer, and those who are acquainted with that breed of people know that Mainers have a fierce attachment to ancestral roots, but that they bring incredible talents, often not recognized by others, to their lives and that of others. So it was with Roger Luce. What I didn't know in Darien was that he was a native of Newburgh ME (near Bangor) and that his family had owned and occupied Butternut Hill Gardens for nearly two centuries before him. So focused was he on that little community that his 1947 Master's Thesis from the University of ME was a history of the public schools in Newburgh, ME which, if I am not mistaken, never made it to the *New York Times* Best Seller list. The property fell to him, and that was where he returned after leaving Darien.

But Roger didn't just return to Maine. He returned with a theory of plants. His lifetime passion was flowers, especially magnolias and azaleas. But he wasn't just interested in colors and smells; he had the particular goal of hybridizing these flowers to make them more hardy so that they would grow further north in Maine. While we might think this as insignificant, it really was enormously significant, both aesthetically and scientifically, since it really was a quest to extend beauty ever further north. His efforts were greeted with success so that at his death in 2002 he was recognized as one of the handful of most influential Maine master gardeners of his generation. One of the ways this recognition happened was that an azalea hybrid was even named after him. Here is a link to a picture of the "Azalea Roger Luce," halfway down the page: https://fernwoodnursery.wordpress.com/tag/azalea-roger-luce/

And, in 2022 this name was added to the International Rhododendron Register: https://azaleas.org/.../Azaleas_Registered_in_2022.pdf

I am so glad that I learned about Roger's post-Darien accomplishments, and I would much rather think of him as the "King of Magnolias," his nickname in ME, than as the guy who dished out demerits to me at Middlesex Junior High in 1966.

C. Running for Office

Sept. 4, 2024

One activity that proved more memorable for me at Middlesex Junior High than expected was running for student body treasurer (1966-67). I came from a numbers-oriented family, and so it was kind of expected that I would like to add and subtract numbers, and I thought that was what a student body treasurer did. In this post I will describe my campaign for that office as a fourteen year-old.

Even at the Junior High level one had to campaign, however ineptly. The primary means of doing so was hanging posters of various sizes around the halls urging people to vote for you. Most were straightforward: "Vote for Long" or somewhat inane, such as having a guy bursting out of a pool with water dripping down him with the caption: "Come Clean: Vote Long." But with my older brother's help I managed to develop a poster that even got the "authorities" involved.

The "authority" I mention here was not Mr. Luce. I have written about him previously, and I think he considered it "beneath" him to police campaigns. That task was given to Mr. Willoughby, a short, somewhat stout counselor. Indeed he was my guidance counselor. We only met once, and I still remember his first question to me because it shocked me. He looked at me and said, "Well, Mr. Long, how is the operation going?" He was trying to ask me about my schoolwork, but I panicked briefly, felt my body and said, "What operation?"—as if they had performed a lobotomy on me unawares. In any case, we got Mr. Willoughby unwittingly involved in my campaign.

My older brother was in high school and had discovered girls, and he decided that a poster with a kind of sexual overtone (or undertone) would help me out. He had also recently discovered, probably not from personal experience, the verb "lay" in its relational meaning. So, he had me cut out a picture of a pretty woman in a semi-seductive pose from Life or Look or one of the magazines of the day, and then we composed a caption, which we wrote in red magic marker: "Lay" (and the word was in quotation marks) .... "Lay" down the Law, and Vote for Long ... That was all it said, and then the picture of the woman was under it.

Because we knew that Mr. Willoughby was the enforcer, we decided to hang it in a prominent position, but hang it 8' above the ground. We, strapping 6-footers, could barely reach that high to hang it, but we knew it would be above Mr. Willoughby's reach. So, there it was. Day by day I went by it, smiling. Kids mostly ignored it, but a few got a chuckle out of my poster.

Well, the word got back to Mr. Willoughby about it and one day, when the hall was nearly empty but I happened to be in it, I saw him standing under my poster. He knew he had to take it down. But I saw him reach up, clipboard in hand, and he couldn't get to it. So, he lay down his clipboard and tried to jump up. Still, too short. He tried more heroically to jump, but again to no avail. Then, he gave my poster one last look, waved his hands at it in frustration, as if to say, "Well, no one will ever really know," and then left.

And the conclusion of the story is that no one ever really knew—until this post.

D. From Darien, Connecticut to Atherton, California in 1967

August 21, 2024

I was delighted to hear people's experiences with graduation speakers in Darien after I related my family story of the 1946 graduation (the year my mother graduated from DHS). I wanted to continue my life story very briefly here because someone asked me about it. I want especially to recreate the world of 1967, the year my family moved from Darien to the San Francisco Bay Area.

The point I will make is that I experienced "culture shock" three years before the concept was popularized by Alvin Toffler (in his 1970 book of that same title).

My family had been a CT and NY family since the 17th century. My father, however, was transferred from the home office of Metropolitan Life Insurance Company in summer 1967 to head up the Data Processing (as it was then called) of the company in San Francisco. We left in August, 1967, driving our Ford Station Wagon, Connecticut Plate 603 909. They chose an elite little town to move to--Atherton CA, next to Palo Alto and Menlo Park--and I began as a sophomore at Menlo-Atherton HS.

It was the so called "Summer of Love" when I arrived in the Bay Area. I ruefully remarked twenty years later that I had little previous experience either of "summer" or "love" in my upbringing in Darien, even though I was starting to explore relational complexities, mostly through 9th grade parties thrown by girls in my social group. These parties were the "cleanest" parties you could imagine, with the raciest things being brushing against each other in a game of Twister.

But I arrived in San Francisco, then, as a kind of innocent Darien-bred teen, in the Summer of Love. Music, and tons of it, was everywhere. I knew I was in a different world. For example, Lindsey Buckingham, of the future Fleetwood Mac, lived three doors down in my affluent neighborhood, though he had just graduated from the high school. Yet, I was thrown into this new and strange world. I couldn't believe it. The boys wore jeans in school and didn't wear ties to church. Long hair was common on boys, and a certain odor in the air which I never previously experienced seemed to waft over me wherever I went. People thought that my "straightness" meant I was from Nebraska, and so the rumors started that I was a farm boy who was behind the times.

I confirmed those rumors through one memorable encounter that will end this post. I was once accosted by an upperclassman, long flowing hair, bell-bottom pants, beads dangling from pants and shirt, a kind of hazy distance in his eyes, who stopped me at school one day and simply asked me, "Hey, man, got some grass?" I, sort of terrified and taken off my guard, simply responded, "No, but I mow it in the summer." My journey of what I felt was terminal nerddom was beginning.

21

Basil Gildersleeve and the Invention of the Ph. D. Program in America

THIS IS A MORE SPECULATIVE HISTORICAL essay or, better said, notes for such an essay, derived from knowledge and study of the history of American higher education, the Civil War, American Presbyterianism, and the development of instruction in the Classics in American colleges in the mid-nineteenth century. It just has some of the "bones" of something that someday might turn into an essay, but it is valuable in showing how ideas germinate for me and how knowledge of several fields leads to speculation that may someday be fruitful …

On Basil Gildersleeve and the Development of the American Ph. D. Degree
August 21, 2024

The following is an email I sent to Prof. Andrew Berns, who had earlier sent me a copy of Gildersleeve's (1831-1924) 1879 article on classical philology and the American university. I just have a list of somewhat desultory thoughts here, but I thought of a way to put Gildersleeve's article into the context of the growth of the American Ph. D. degree. My email is here:

Andrew: What really interested me about your email was Gildersleeve's article. I could put the thoughts into a longer essay than you would expect, but I will be mercifully brief. The thing that most interested me about Gildersleeve was not any personal "meaning" his essay might have for my life but about how it tells me a huge amount about the social history of the university in the mid-late nineteenth century and the development of the Ph. D. degree in America. Just a few words. If I were writing an essay I would lay out:

1. The Growth of the Research University model after the Napoleonic Wars in Germany beginning about 1820.
2. The "rediscovery" of the Greek classics in Germany starting at the end of the 18th century and picking up steam in the 19th century. Goethe was responsible in many ways for this.
3. The particular universities which cultivated this idea. They would have been three: 1) Berlin--the "Humboldt" University, founded in 1810. 2) Surprisingly the second would have been Bonn, which became the "nonsectarian" school of the Rhineland, and focused on classics as well as more modern subjects. "Refounded" about 1820. 3) Then, Gottingen became the place where ultimately the "History of Religions" school developed later in the 19th century, which transformed the study of early Christianity in its Greco-Roman Context.
4. Now we move to Gildersleeve. He had the unique experience of studying at ALL THREE of these German universities, from 1850-1853, getting his Ph. D. from Gottingen. So, he perfectly imbibed this strange, new and utterly exciting new world of the "research university" with classical philology as its basis for him.

Note: two of his American contemporaries at Gottingen wrote the two most notable "scientific" grammars of ancient Greek in English in America ... Smyth and Goodwin, and both of their books are still available, and perhaps even used today!..thus, the "Germanification" of ancient Greek study happened in America beginning in about the 1870s.

5. But the idea of the Ph. D. was slow to come to America. Yale had awarded a Ph. D. in 1861, but then the Civil War came and there really wasn't much cultural support for the concept until the 1870s.
6. The person around whom that support would coalesce was Daniel Coit Gilman, who would be the founding president of Johns Hopkins in Baltimore in 1876. He came in with a vision of making Hopkins the first research university, on the German model, in America.
7. Guess what one of his first hiring decisions was? To hire Gildersleeve away from the U of Va, where he had been for 20 years. Gildersleeve came to Hopkins in 1876, and was actually Gilman's first hire. Gildersleeve's motto, after the relative obscurity at VA, was borrowed from Descartes and, ultimately, from Ovid: "Bene vixit, bene qui latuit," –"He has lived well who has hid (himself) well." Also, he had a saying about classicists: The English were pedants; the French were too elegant, but the Germans were thorough."
8. Now, Gildersleeve was going to give the intellectual heft behind the growing concept of an American research university. After all, he SAW it repeatedly in his German sojourn. The first Ph. D.'s awarded by Hopkins were in 1878, but the idea was still developing.
9. Note that Gildersleeve wrote this article in 1879. One way to read it, of course, is just a paean to the virtue of the kind of classical philology and word stories/histories that I love in any language, but now you see why I am enthralled by Gildersleeve's article. It is, in a way, the Magna Carta of

> the concept of the Ph. D. … applied of course to Classical Philology.

So, I may have 'overread' the evidence, which I tend to do in my exuberance, but I see a direct connection from the "re-founding" of German universities in the 1820s, to Gildersleeve's unique experience in Germany in the early 1850s, to his coming to Johns Hopkins, to the efflorescence of the American Ph. D., to this article in 1879.

I am repulsed, of course, by some of Gildersleeve's views on slavery and race, but his role in defining this "new thing" called the research university hasn't, I believe, fully been told. First draft here!

22

So, What Ails America and Americans?

June 26, 2024

THERE REALLY IS NO REASON, FROM the data alone, why such high levels of discontent should be registering in American society these days. Jobs are available, though admittedly it seemingly is getting more difficult to find an easy "match" between skills sought and skills possessed by applicants. But even if you don't find work, there are frequently ample programs for the homeless or those out of work. The stock market is hitting all-time highs seemingly every other day, and the 50% or so of Americans who have investments in stocks or bonds are seeing their portfolios shine as never before. Families have fewer children and more dogs, thus providing more stable and enjoyable family structures than in previous generations. Most signs, then, seem to point to high levels of satisfaction in American life.

Yet, surveys consistently show higher levels of discontent among all ages of Americans than ever before. This dissatisfaction manifests itself in disquiet with almost every formerly trusted institution in American life, as well as complaints about political affiliations and activities of neighbors, family members and others in the community. People are less and less tolerant of political differences with others. Obesity is on the rise as well as the health concerns accompanying it. Drug use, both legal and illegal, has never been higher. America is drugged, obese, dissatisfied, hyper-religious (an issue I discuss in other essays), rich and fully dissatisfied. What is to blame and what might be a way out of the dilemma?

The dual culprits, in my mind, are historical and philosophical. That is, we are plagued because we are thinking a thought that is damaging us (philosophy) and we are part of a process that seemingly has us trapped in debilitating ways (history). Let me explain each briefly. The philosophical issue can be called a too vigorous belief in the promise of the American dream. That "dream," long existing in American culture, was neatly defined by James Truslow Adams in a 1931 book, *The Epic of America,* and his definition stressed not simply the hope, but really the expectation that Americans possess, that their lives would be richer, fuller, more meaningful and more fun than that of their parents. It is almost an American birthright to believe this. When Adams articulated the theory in 1931, he suggested that this expectation was probably to be realized over the course of one's lifetime. Yet, the insidious nature of this idea as it develops further in our day is that young people still believe in the American dream but they want it to be realized for them THIS YEAR or NEXT YEAR. But this can't and won't happen.

What makes the expectation so insidious for people of our time is that hope in the American dream comes just as the baby boomers are cashing in on the system in ways never before experienced just because of their lives as baby-boomers. What this means is that the baby boomers not only believed in the American dream but really set up the system so that the maximum benefits economically would flow to them rather than to their children or others. An example is how union contracts of the 1960s and 1970s, which actually became the model for many private industry contracts, were so "loaded" with benefits that, as it were, all the money was "gone" by the time we got to 2000. State government workers salary and benefit packages, for example, were so "loaded" that they sometimes have hurt the system for subsequent workers. And example is the Oregon PERS (Public Employee Retirement System) system. Formerly if one was a "Tier 1" employee one got a rich array of salary and benefits that was so generous that a person could retire with a retirement package well exceeding his/her salary during work life. This is an example, and an indication of how the 'experiment" to support workers in those days was so generous that there was little money left for workers once the years 2000 and later came.

Thus, we are in the interesting position now of having loads more money but it is almost all going to retired people or people who own stock in companies which are profitable. Those who are now in their most productive years are therefore the most frustrated. Unless the parents, that is, the baby boomers born between about 1946-1964, support their children, even if very successful, the children's life cannot measure up economically to that of their parents. And, when this is combined with the philosophical expectation, given to the younger people by the American Dream, that they will have MORE, it just is too difficult to endure. Depression, anxiety, obesity, anger and all kinds of conflict then ensues, and life is miserable, increasingly for young people in their 30s and 40s.

Thus, even though this was just presented as a philosophical issue, it is both philosophical and economic. The two were wedded about 50 years ago to provide a most rosy and attractive system for the baby boomers . Later generations have not been as fortunate and baby boomers, in general, just don't understand it. This causes immense rifts between the generations, which may manifest itself in political differences or just increasing tension in families.

But then, when this is married to a historical concern, it almost always sinks the boats of Gen X's Y's and Millennials or whatever other letters come later. The historical concern is that the world is still controlled by long-lived baby boomers, who are unwilling to step down to let the "next gens" define the issues as they see them and take charge. A case in point is the American Presidential election of 2024, where octogenarians and near octogenarians are fighting it out to rule in irrelevance for four more years in America. We SHOULD be making intelligent transitions in leadership now, but we aren't. Thus, it will be, as I have argued or stated in a poem of mine, a very rough landing for our society when the baby boomers finally have power pried from their hands.

So, the "next gens" have every reason to be livid about things. The baby boomers, who always were told they were special, now think they are the most special generation imaginable, but they are stealing the resources, polluting the planet, not letting the reins of power go and basically undermining their children and perhaps their grandchildren in life. That is why the discontent is so high in America.

And, what is the solution? It is multi-factorial, but not as difficult as one might first imagine. But, I don't think I will lay it out here. Enough has been said for sharp people to infer an answer.

23
A Bundle of isms

I HAD A POPULAR WEBSITE FROM ABOUT 2003-2012, just as websites were beginning to proliferate. I posted more than 4,000 of my essays in this decade, but I also presented other genres of writing on that site. I entitled one of those genres "Billphorisms," which are nothing more than "aphorisms" by "Bill." I published about 500 of them in those years; those below represent about 10% of them. I still try to come up with proverbial-type statements to capture the seriousness, and humor, of life. Some of these are factually-based; some are imagined. I borrowed a few from a friend in the South; I borrowed a few from online sources; most of them, however, originated with me.

A. Palindromic headline about an assault on a man who didn't pay child support:
"Deadbeat Dad Beat Dead"

B. *Pro se* defendant seeks a delay when appearing before a court and says:
"May it please the court. Defendant asks for an arraign check."

C. Self-description of man who knows he has completely angered his wife.
"I am in term oil."

D. Headline:
"Sustainability Expert Convicted of Illegal Dumping"

E. Headline:
"Camouflaged Army Vehicle Disappears"

F. Headline:
"One-armed man Applauds the Kindness of Strangers"

G. Poster Mistake:
Instead of "You ought to explore Marital Counseling" it said "You ought to explore Martial Counseling." Any difference?

H. Headline:
"Expert Witness Testifies that Teen Pregnancy Plummets after Age 20."

I. Headline:
"Longevity Consultant Dies at 25"

J. Headline:
"Dead Body Found in Cemetery."

K. Headline:
"Seventeen Dead in Morgue Shooting Spree"

L. Headline:
"Slowdown Continues to Accelerate"

M. Headline:
"Hydration Expert Drowns"

N. Headline:
"Phisher Scammed!"

O. Article Title:
"Large-Breasted Woman's Bible Study adopts new name: 'Bustier than Thou.'"

P. Sign outside of Breast Enhancement Clinic:
"Create a Mammary."

Q. Sign outside a Church: "Totally Blessed"
Sign outside a Spa: "Totally Blissed"
Sign outside a Bar: "Totally Blitzed"

R. Shocking Headline:
"Invasive Species Retreat"

S. Wise Saying:
"Old Upholsterers Never Die. They Always Recover"

T. Headline,
"Miracle Cure Kills Fifth Patient"

U. Headline,
"Something Went Wrong in Jet Crash, Expert Surmises"

V. Headline:
"Planetary Scientist Urges Probe to Uranus"

W. Quote:
"When the astronaut was lost in space, the only thing left to do was to write his orbituary."

X. Heard in a sermon:
"We must get rid of the scrounge of racism."

Y. Musings of seniors:
"Well, Elmer is now in his anecdotage."

Z. Quote:
"He is beyond the ultimate. I would call him the penultimate."

AA. After I displayed dazzling memory a secretary asked me, "So are you telling me you have a photogenic memory?"

BB. "I am against gay marriage because of the sacredness of the union," he solemnly explained to his third wife.

CC. Reflecting on the life of Coach Pat Summit of Tennessee women's basketball, "With a coach named Summit, where else could they go but to the top?"

DD. Reflecting on the Eagles' tune "Lyin' Eyes":
"The Eagles were Celebrities. There ain't no way to hide their lionize."

EE. Reflections on teaching great literature:
"Dante is daunting, but you can always hit it out of the park with Homer."
"Job is a real job."
"Some may consider Euripides a minor playwright, but no one says Aeschylus Smeshchylus."

FF. A Drywaller's favorite Arthur Conan Doyle story:
"The Spackled Band."

GG. Course Title of an Environmental Law Class Taught by a Feminist Professor
"The Engendered Species Act."

HH. My friend used to lecture on the evils of circumcision. Now he has retired. He is an inactive intactivist.

II. I was disturbed when my New Hampshire friend seemed to take everything for granite.

JJ. Carl Linnaeus (1707-78), the Father of Taxonomy, wrote his autobiography five times over the course his life. The only thing in the universe he apparently couldn't classify was himself.

KK. Signs on the Oregon coast warn beachcombers to beware of 'Sneaker Waves.' Sure enough, within minutes a soggy pair of Nike's washed ashore.

LL. An elitist with respect to words might look down on someone for whom tintinnabulation doesn't ring a bell.

MM. It is ironic that the English word meaning "rule by women" has an acute accent on the antepenult.

NN. The professor told the student that his very poor paper was simply abdominal.

OO. What the grad student never imagined was that there was so much acidemia in academia.

PP. Divagate means "to wander about." It has nothing to do with a scandal among prima donnas.

QQ. Spoken by a geology student after finding an astonishingly beautiful rock:
"Holy Schist!"

RR. A heated argument between two architectural historians inside a Cathedral:
The first architect: "Watch it or I will kick you in the *apse.*"
The response of the second: "If you do, you and your *buttocks* will go *flying.*"
The first: "Don't be *na(i)ve.* You will be thrown *clere* over the third *story.*"
Final response: "(De)*fenestration* for you."

SS. Reflecting on Jesus' Words: "Man doesn't live by bread alone. He needs cliches."

TT. "A sure sign that people have lost their creative edge is they say they want to think OUTSIDE THE BOX."

UU. A Sexual Primer on New York State geography:
"First you come to Howe Caverns; then you go to the Finger Lakes and finally you don't want to miss Viagra Falls."

VV. If Jesus' condemner had been into aerobics, he would have been called PONTIUS PILATES.

WW. A friend bought me a shirt for Christmas that really ENHANDSOMES me.

XX. A friend suggested I visit the Cranberry Museum in SW Washington but, frankly, I didn't want to get bogged down there. So, instead, I got hung up in the barbed wire museum in La Crosse KS.

YY. And then there's the all-too-familiar story of the turf wars in the Intermountain Grass Growers Association.

ZZ. The literary critic was delighted to land a teaching position in Synecdoche, New York.

AAA. The Priest was happy to become Chaplain in the Sacramental Airport.

BBB. Actual conversation with my mother: "Mom, I just finished my autobiography." Her response, "Great. Who is it about?"

CCC. Actual Names of people in Real Jobs … or maybe they are fake:
A Justice on King's Bench in the 1610s: Justice Crook
A Dentist in Oregon: Dr Payne
A Funeral Director: Mr Coffin
A Paver of Roads: Mr. Street
A Chiropractor: Dr. Popp
An Orthopedic Surgeon: Dr. Bonebrake
An Obstetrician: Dr. Buster Hyman
A Spelunker: Ms. Caverna Cave
Famous Obesity Researcher: Prof. Ima Hogg
The Language Instructor: Dr. Rosetta Stone

DDD. A little-known common law writ requiring court appearance of dumb people: HABEAS DOOFUS

EEE. A Common Complaint among crime investigators: "Is there METH in his MADNESS?"

FFF. Theological Reflection on Creation, "And on the Eighth Day, God Created ADVIL."

GGG. "And then there's the story of the cereal killer who murdered for Special K"

HHH. Reflection on Christmas Gifts: "If I receive one more calendar for a present featuring the work of Impressionist Painters, I will start throwing watering cans at Gothic Cathedrals."

III. Meet the Famous Weeping Armenian Gentleman, "Mr. Arman Boohoogian."

JJJ. The Scholar took a Deep Dive into the History of Shallow Thinking

KKK. It's ironic that the English word for "single-syllable word" has five syllables.

LLL. Thomas Hobbes managed to escape most of the particulars of his famous definition of life: "Solitary, poor, nasty, brutish and short."

MMM. One of the more delicious ironies of the English language is that the OED tells us that the word *orthoepy* can be pronounced five different ways.

NNN. He knew that his ministry among prostitutes was destined to fail when the first hymn they requested to be sung was:
"All The Way My Savior Leads Me"

OOO. Likewise, his ministry among paraplegics collapsed when he suggested they sing:
"Stand Up, Stand Up for Jesus!"

PPP. He failed likewise with dentists when they only wanted to sing,
"Crown Him with Many Crowns"

QQQ. And he finally abandoned ministry altogether when the conference title for narcissists he was planning was entitled:
"Salvation: It's All about You."

24

Something is Bothering Me

September 28, 2024

VERY FEW PEOPLE REALLY "SPOOK" OR scare me. I look on with complete placidity while an obviously deranged person screams two feet away from me. I just look him in the eyes and ask him calmly if something is the matter—and invariably he quiets down. I see people loaded down with all kinds of weaponry, and I quietly just pass by them or strike up a nonchalant conversation. I run into conspiracy theorists with wild looks in their eyes and confident, but usually incoherent, words about how we are on the brink of societal collapse, and I simply and quietly ask them to recite some of the things on which they rely for their wild prognostications. But the one group that destabilizes me almost completely are those religious folk, mostly about my age, who speak with ease about God's purpose in the universe and God's perfect ordering of all things. They seem to have a direct pipeline to the divine heart and act as if they are mere mouthpieces for God as they interpret all kinds of events that have or are about to happen in the universe. I seem to be particularly vulnerable to letting this kind of person affect me because, for years, I wasn't so far away from them in my confident speech about divine purposes. But now I can't speak with much authority on the "Almighty's Purposes," to quote our sixteenth President in his Second Inaugural.

Let me tell you about two guys, a little older than I, whose confident speech on divine purposes does nothing but confuse, and even scare, me. Let's call them Tim and John. Both of them are in their mid-70s and are ardent believers in the utter and triumphant clarity of the divine purposes in the world. From all external measures, they aren't impressive people but, to their credit, as they stressed to me, they worship an Impressive God. Well, Tim led a Bible study I attended a while back, and he confidently dished out interpretations for which the word "harebrained" would be much too kind. He grew up Catholic in a rough Catholic neighborhood outside of Boston but was "saved" (which probably means he ran into a Protestant Fundamentalist Evangelist while he was in his early 20s) and then devoted himself to a life as a woodworker. He hated government but ended up working for it for his entire career because the pay and benefits were so good. He wanted to learn all about the Bible but he said that, after much prayer, God told him not to go to college. God was so terribly real for him but God seemed to give him answers to his prayers that were not only startlingly clear but were so definitively contrary or diametrically opposed to the obvious answers God "gave" me (i.e., go to college and get your degrees you dummy, Bill) that I was feeling that perhaps I made a bad choice.

I thought a bit about his life. I felt that state governments weren't perfect, but they really tried to take care of their workers and should be commended. He disagreed, but didn't mind taking his money from them. We studied 1st Peter, where the author purports to write "from Babylon," which almost unanimously is received by scholars as a kind of "wink, wink" hint that he is writing from Rome, but Tim doggedly argued for Peter's Babylon sojourn. When I asked him to construct a chronology of Peter's life that would have allowed such a thing, he looked at me blankly as if it was impertinent of me to ask him a question. He then blithely re-asserted his belief. I think I was destabilized by someone like this because, in my "elitist" upbringing, I would just have considered such a person dumb both by choice (no college) and by natural endowment (wasn't the brightest bulb …), but because God fully encased Tim's life, I began to worry that he might indeed have some kind of special access to ultimate truth where learning is actually a disadvantage and where learning how to speak and reason clearly is just such a pain. Thus, he was able unskillfully to dismiss everything I said because he had God. And God was so real, so close, so communicative to him. I just had to admire, and fear, it a little. If I were simply a sociologist I would say that he was a product of a "pahk the cah" Boston accent, a lower-middle Catholic culture where its men worked for the wealthier Protestant men who owned businesses and ran the government and universities, but because he had God guiding him in everything, I became scared, and I didn't know how to handle it.

A second case in point is John. He is different from Tim in that he wasn't a Catholic growing up but he was born and nurtured as a Protestant in pre-statehood Alaska, giving him a kind of frontier roughness that many would call uncouth, were it not for the fact that he was really close to God, too. Well, he decided he wanted to go to college and study languages—having a kind of knack for learning about other cultures, but something kept happening to him and he eventually had to drop out of college with no degree, despite the fact that God was with him. He knocked around for years, finally landing a job as an assistant librarian at some Christian college that probably told him it was such a privilege to work for them that they didn't feel they should pay him much. John dutifully went along, amassing some impressive knowledge of extremely arcane things. He wasn't a teacher of the Bible, but he did, now that I think of it, have far more answers than questions about most things in life.

But he realized in mid-career that he didn't have any money or credentials, though he had a vibrant relationship with God, and so he began to try on lots of hats. He thought he would become a writer but never got around to writing. He played a good guitar but couldn't get it together to record anything. He befriended a retired medical person who wanted to be a poet and told him he would help edit and publish his poems. The medical person, also a real believer, was about 100 pounds overweight, and I cautioned him to lose some, but God was with him, too, even though his poems were sometimes pretty nasty attacks on Muslims, as I recall. Well, the poet ended up dying and John was left with his poems, but hasn't yet gotten around to editing them. When I saw John last he looked haggard, for he is caring for his wife, who now is spiraling into dementia and it seemingly is taking a toll on John too. His face brightened, however, when he told me he has so much hope for the future. Why, I asked him? Well, during the Pandemic, which he doesn't believe existed, when he caught a disease which didn't also exist, America was flooded with 3,000,000 immigrants. Rather than wanting to MAGA them, he thought this was a great opportunity to bring Jesus to them.

I gently excused myself from him to return to my own work. I was fully destabilized by the confident tales of those two who know that God is RIGHT THERE but whose lives are, from my limited and obviously benighted perspective, unattractive. Their ideas make no sense to me. Their reasons for clinging to the "old rugged cross" are not at all persuasive to me. They scare me because if they are right about God, which they know they are, I am in such deep shit!

25

When do Hell and Heaven Begin?

August 17, 2024

I AM IN A PHASE OF MY life where I am trying to re-examine theological concepts I adopted and even eagerly embraced in younger days. One thing I accepted was the true and actual reality of a Heaven of bliss and a Hell of torment. I deal with that issue below, but my major focus in this essay is the simple question of when Heaven and Hell begin for people. The questions are quite natural and even important, since if there is such a glorious place as Heaven and a dismal place as Hell, it might be nice to know when you actually get to one or the other place and when the love or heat is turned on. After all, if the beginning of these things has to await some future event which itself is repeatedly put off or delayed or unrealized, then there becomes quite a concern about whether this glorious or sad future will ever be realized. And, in the meantime, one is just sitting there (or probably lying there) cooling one's heels or, better said, probably unconscious, waiting for things to work themselves out so that the party or torment can begin.

With these questions issues in mind, let's first phrase the question, then look at a text or two and then quit. When does Hell begin? Some might say that it has already begun in this life for people who live miserable lives, whether of their own manufacture or not. The misery quotient for some people is so high, either because of poverty, illness, conflict or relational strife, that one might be justified in saying that Hell has already begun for them. But then, when you read a passage like Mark 9:43-48, which speaks about worms not dying and fires not being quenched, you see that Jesus was playing for much higher stakes in describing Hell than simply the multiform anxieties of living in this world. For Jesus in this passage (and he spent six whole verses just reiterating the same idea three times), Hell is a place of immense torment. The worms will crawl in and crawl out, and the fire that consumes a person will not go out. The degree of immense suffering to be experienced by those in Hell is so great that I am sure that Jesus hoped the prospect of it would so scare the Bejesus out of people they would turn to him.

But the use of scare or threat techniques to encourage "coming to faith" seems to be ethically suspect and practically useless. If I go to a Toyota car dealership and then don't want a Toyota, and I tell the guy I think I will go over to the Mazda dealership, he doesn't threaten me with Hell and eternal punishment. He wishes me a good day, realizing that the nature of capitalist society is that people have choices. But, if one even hints at the fact that one might not want freely to choose the way of Christ, one is threatened with the most immense, permanent and painful punishments. The most unimaginable suffering is being prepared for those who reject the kindness of God. If we are raising children and one or more happen to go astray, our love for them never dies and we probably will bless them always in our prayers and thoughts. But if God, who seemingly loves us much more than human parents love children, easily can confine numerous millions to eternal suffering because they happen not to acknowledge in the right way a 'gift' he sent them, a gift that may never have clearly been presented to them in the first place, well, how can we parents be justified in continuing to love our children that may have "strayed" from the "good path?"

We should probably hate them, too, if we truly want to follow the example of God. We then would be about the dumbest people on this planet if we were to keep loving our children, since God doesn't seem to have a problem consigning millions of His children to utterly painful and permanent torment for rejecting him. So, this kind of activity by God isn't very admirable to me. It isn't something I want to imitate either with people who might not be open to what I have to say or sell or with my kids who might disagree with me.

Nevertheless, Jesus spends six verses in Mark 9 talking about the need to cut off or extrude bodily appendages or organs if they cause us to sin (hand, foot, eye). We probably shouldn't take this passage literally, because getting rid of a hand or foot or eye is pretty serious stuff and we don't see many people walking around with stumps or bandages over the eyes as a result of self-inflicted injuries for the sake of cultivating personal holiness.

So, we have an immense problem with the concept of WHO gets to Hell, according to Jesus, but the real question I started probing earlier is WHEN this Hell (and Heaven) begins. If it doesn't begin in this life it has to begin either at the point of death, at a point that is a definite, but unspecified, time after death or at a decisive event at an unspecified future time (like the Last Judgment). Let's take them *seriatim.* If one immediately at death suffers the pains of Hell (and, by extension), the joys of Heaven, then the dying moment is everything, and one doesn't have a moment's gap in consciousness. One is immediately translated into this other realm. This seems highly unlikely, for it would mean that at the funeral/memorial service, the person either is dancing and praising God or is in utter torment. Nothing that can be done at the service affects one whit the reality that the person now feels and really seems quite irrelevant. But this notion of immediate conscious awareness of Heaven or Hell seems so far-fetched that I can't give it credence.

Well, how about ten minutes after death? Or, how about a year, which is the time after most people have forgotten about you anyway? Perhaps the great transfer comes after God lets you stay in the ground for a year. Perhaps it took some time to process all the deaths and sometimes, especially if there is a heavenly Pandemic, there might be a staff shortage to keep records up to date. So, since God is a God who gets things done and doesn't just wait around with millions of his faithful doing squat until some future time, we might suggest that Heaven and Hell begin "after a time." Not long, but long enough to give a kind of "break" between the two worlds. But other than this solution having no warrant at all in any text or tradition, this makes it seem that the reason for delay in Heaven had to do with deficiencies in Heavenly accounting software. Yet, many people have the experience of talking to departed loved ones or receiving reports from the other realm telling about the condition of loved ones. This is intriguing, but it is hard to build a doctrinal framework around these reports.

So, the final choice is that Heaven and Hell begin (or, the conscious feeling and experience of those two realities) at a definite time in the distant (or near) future, which might be known as the Great Judgment Day of God. This is the day when all the accounts are finally settled, when the video tapes of your life are readily accessible on interlibrary loan from the Heavenly archives, and you can see all those dastardly things you have done or thought, as well as whether you "checked the right boxes" by claiming Christ as your Savior to save your sorry ass from the Hell that is being richly prepared for millions of unsuspecting and sometimes unrepentant creatures. So, you who have properly signed on the Heavenly dotted line will be ushered into unending bliss, though the full scope of activities available to you in Heaven is somewhat unclear. Most people would find that constant singing in the Heavenly choir is kind of boring, but God may so transform minds that this becomes a most joyous obligation. But, Heaven may consist of other blessed things—maybe you liked to fish, and now you will have a well-stocked pond while you are always in the shade. Maybe you like to hunt, and heaven might be full of all kinds of slow-moving and vulnerable beasts you can kill. But, then again, if beasts can't die in Heaven, maybe you can shoot them repeatedly and have the sense of eternal joy because you can kill them so many times and get credit for it, but they won't die, and so you get to keep doing it.

I am getting a bit far afield, but this is the theory that Heaven (and Hell) only begins on that Last Day—the Judgment Day—when the Heavens will be rolled up like a scroll, when God will finally not have to put up with any more guff from anyone. But, the only problem is that this Judgment Day may never come. Oh, the true believers will tell you that it is right around the corner and that eternity is a long time compared to the short waiting time for the Day of Judgment, but what about if you have a hard time believing it will truly come … and you are right? What if Jesus was just a bit too eager in his preaching 2000 years ago and, when he talked about these things happening (i.e., widespread destruction, which probably was going to usher in the Last Days) in his generation he was actually wrong. Oops, I was trained never to say a statement like that, but what if Jesus actually was wrong? What about, too, if the whole concept of a day of ultimate judgment and reckoning is just more of a figment of literary (or sci-fi) imagination, coming mostly from a book (Revelation) not known for its ability to touch down to earth in any practical way once you get to 4:1?

So, now that I bring this essay to a close, I do so with the sense that I am almost worse off than when I began. I don't believe that Heaven/Hell begin at death. I don't believe that they begin a bit further down the line when God has had a chance to "process" all the deaths and sort people out. I don't believe that there will be a great Judgment Day in the future. So, it never begins, really, for me. But, I am safe because I have accepted Jesus as Savior and Lord. I am SAFE. Phew. God can't do anything about that anymore or He would be untrue to His promise. Can't do that. So, I am safe. And that makes me feel not a whit happier.

Made in the USA
Monee, IL
23 July 2025

21753931R00094